RAISED BY PUPPETS

Only to Be Killed by Research

Also by Andrei Codrescu

POETRY

License to Carry a Gun (1970)
The History of the Growth of Heaven (1971, 1973)
the, here, what, where (1972)
Secret Training (1973)
A Serious Morning (1973)
grammar & money (1973)
A Mote Suite for Jan & Anselm (1976)
The Lady Painter (1977)
The Marriage of Insult & Injury (1977)
For the Love of a Coat (1978)
Necrocorrida (1980)
Diapers on the Snow (1981)
Selected Poems 1970–1980 (1983)
Comrade Past & Mister Present (1986)

FICTION

Why I Can't Talk on the Telephone (1971)
The Repentance of Lorraine (1976)
Monsieur Teste in America & Other Instances of Realism (1987)

ESSAYS

A Craving for Swan (1986)

MEMOIRS

The Life & Times of an Involuntary Genius (1975)
In America's Shoes (1983)

TRANSLATIONS

For Max Jacob (1974)
At the Court of Yearning: Poems of Lucian Blaga (1989)

WORKS EDITED

American Poetry Since 1970: Up Late (1987)
The Stiffest of the Corpse: An Exquisite Corpse Reader (1989)

RAISED BY PUPPETS

Only to Be Killed by Research

ANDREI CODRESCU

ADDISON-WESLEY PUBLISHING COMPANY, INC.
Reading, Masachusetts   Menlo Park, California   New York
Don Mills, Ontario   Wokingham, England   Amsterdam   Bonn
Sydney   Singapore   Tokyo   Madrid   San Juan

Author's Note: These essays were broadcast on National Public Radio's "All Things Considered" between 1986 and 1988. Some of them appeared in a slightly different form in my "Penny Post" column on the Op-Ed page of the *Baltimore Sun* during the same period.

The lines by Lawrence Ferlinghetti on page 13 are from the poem "Lost Parents," included in his collection *Wild Dreams of a New Beginning,* published by New Directions, New York, in 1988.

The sentences by Vincent van Gogh on page 105 are from a letter to his brother Theo dated 3 September 1882, included in *The Complete Letters of Vincent van Gogh,* published by New York Graphic Society, Boston, MA, in 1958.

Library of Congress Cataloging-in-Publication Data

Codrescu, Andrei, 1946–
   Raised by puppets, only to be killed by
research.

   I. Title.
PS3553.03R35 1989   814'.54   88-8064
ISBN 0-201-12183-2

Cover design by Copenhaver Cumpston
Text design by Patricia Dunbar
Set in 10-point Palatino by Total Concept Associates, Brattleboro, VT

ABCDEFGHIJ-DO-89
First Printing, March 1989

Contents

The author wishes to bow deeply to the following beings who in their various bright ways set him wistfully afire:

TED BERRIGAN (1934–1983)

JEFFREY MILLER (1948–1977)

Radio Piece

My horrible stepfather, who was an engineer, and whose only pleasure in life was building amateur radios, used to spend every weekend at his workshop table, inventing. He invented a phone radio, a clock radio, a butterchurn radio, and a mailbox radio, long before these things became common. So proud was he of his radios that he punished anyone who didn't show the proper degree of amazement before them. Once he beat me for writing dirty words on the world map that hung over his workshop table. He didn't beat me because the words were dirty, but because dirty words distracted him from his radios.

One day I removed a very small piece from inside his latest creation. It took him several cursing days to find out what was wrong. From that time on, I took a little piece out of whatever he was working on every time I chanced by his table. He became horribly moody, and had big fights with my mother. He beat me whenever he could lay his hands on me, which wasn't often: I was too quick, and he was too depressed.

Finally, one day he packed his radios and his bags, and he left us. My mother cried, but it was a great day for me. And now that I have become a little piece in the radio myself, I often wonder if I am not the very first piece that I removed from my horrible stepfather's radio. And whenever somebody says, "I heard one of your radio pieces," a piece of radio comes back to me, removed by little fingers from a mean man's sole pleasure in life.

Who Raised You?

Four young sandhill cranes returned to Wisconsin this summer after spending a year in the wild. As chicks, the cranes were raised by hand puppets that looked like cranes, and then by humans dressed in crane suits. Released into the wild, they had no trouble transferring their attachment from crane dolls and people-cranes to wild cranes.

I was raised by cranes disguised to look like humans. I vaguely remember the desultory chirping that punctuated their crude human sentences. Bent over my crib, they sometimes forgot themselves and chirped unashamed. I had some trouble adjusting to wild humans but at last overcame it in New York City where identities shift as quickly as street corners. Seeing weasels and bobcats hug the walls in Times Square after midnight affirmed my human self in a hurry.

A friend of mine, raised by dogs, wasn't so lucky: as a baby he twice saw the human mask of the German shepherd who was raising him slip. He never quite believed in humans after that: with uncanny acuteness he is able to distinguish the various breeds of dogs among so-called people. He once picked them out of a movie line for me. "Muffy over there," he whispered, "she's a Pomeranian."

I polled my friends and found that most of them too were raised by animals disguised as humans. My pal Volodia, a Soviet émigré, remembered growing up in a zoo. Throughout his childhood and adolescence, he was warned against "imperialist dogs," "putrid capitalist hyenas," and "Trotskyite vultures." Eventually he came to see them everywhere, ready to pounce on the gentler species of comrades among whom he lived. "Have you stopped seeing them?" I asked him. "Yes," he said. "But since I have come to the United States, I have been prey to other animals: 'male chauvinist pigs,' 'stubborn mules,' 'real asses' . . . "

We had a hilarious slide show the other day to which everybody brought family pictures. It was delightful to note how sloppy the human costumes of our parents were. Wolf hairs bristled beneath a poorly pasted-on mustache. A ferret tail was barely camouflaged under a striped spat—a tuft hung out. There were red fox eyes weary behind cheap goggles, rooster combs squished flat but peeking from under ski caps.

There was a time when people weren't ashamed to be seen talking with animals, and animals were not afraid to be seen talking with us. That time was long ago. Since then we have all become endangered species. But a measure of kindness must yet survive between us if we are willing to dress like each other and raise each other again and again.

Too bad we can't do it without masks.

Forgotten Ancestors

My seven-year-old son came home from school with instructions to produce a genealogical chart. "It's OK if your grandfather was hung as a horse thief," he said. "My teacher doesn't care."

Now, it so happens that my grandfather was not. He was killed by a bandit while coming home from his gold mine in the mountains of Transylvania. The bandit put an iron ax through Grandfather's head. (One of my wife's ancestors, however, was not only hanged but drawn and quartered. He was a principal in the beheading of Charles I, King of England. A few years later the Loyalists got him for that.)

My seven-year-old took his teacher at his word. He drew an ax on the half of the large piece of cardboard where my ancestors were supposed to go. He'd have written down Grandfather's name but I don't know it or the names of many other of my forebears. My wife, on the other hand, knows those of every one of hers going back to Adam and Eve. Her family bibles, professional genealogies, and family histories dominate our bookshelves. My family, with the exception of the grandfather axed by the bandit, is lost in murk.

"Just write 'Baron X' in the box for my father's father," I told the kid. My wife, who is a DAR, had him put in all three names of hers.

I racked my brain for other forerunners, but all I found were the gruesome yet noble faces of the pirates in my childhood copy of *Treasure Island* and, when I tried even harder, of the monkeys in my high school biology textbook. It seems my memory of my ancestors is indiscriminate, just as my concept of family is liberal: I accept and embrace anyone willing to join the clan. Perhaps it's all a strange side effect of having sworn away my aristocratic past: I'm a European who took seriously the pledge to renounce all titles to nobility upon becoming an American citizen.

Finally, I had to call my mother. "How about the barons back there?"I said.

"What barons?" she said. "Your ancestors were horse thieves, highwaymen, and mercenaries."

"Were they hanged?" I asked timidly.

"All of them," she said. "As far as I'm concerned."

I said to the kid, "Just put in my father. Your mother's got enough ancestors for the both of us."

Ninja Flu

B oth my sons like to kick down walls. The little one kicks them just hard enough to chip the plaster. The big one shakes the house. The little one has a black stripe on his white karate belt. The big one is a full-rank brown belt. At Halloween and Mardi Gras they go as karate men, only the little one goes as a Ninja. That involves a black kerchief over the face that leaves only the eyes visible, and a variety of weapons including throwing stars, numchucks, staff, sword, poisoned dart, and knife. He knows exactly how to use them because he has videotaped every Japanese Ninja movie ever to hit late-night TV. Some of the movie Ninjas are quite powerful: they breathe fire and leap over buildings and kill thousands single-handedly. Luckily my son's weapons are plastic, and about the Ninjas he is skeptical: "They are probably just ninth-degree black belts," he reports. But it appears that not everybody's as sane as my seven-year-old. Recently a Ninja warrior with a two-and-a-half-foot sword and a fake Oriental accent robbed a gas station in Raytown, Missouri. At the University of Kentucky in Lexington, a lethal Ninja sprayed gunfire into a crowd, wounding two students. And in Los Angeles, two men dressed in Ninja clothes gunned down an elderly couple in cold blood.

We take to fads the way fish take to sushi. American life in the eighties has a decidedly Oriental cast. From fashions to electronics, we wallow in all things Japanese. Pop Zen is the majority religion of young Americans whether they know it or not, and even our seasonal colds come from the Far East. But it is only now, with the emergence of a new type of criminal, that our affinity becomes profound. The East is a fad no more; it is part of our mythical being. Its scrolls have entered the national psyche. The exotic import has become the everyday. The opposite is, no doubt, true about Japan. There, the criminals study John Wayne. Their Ninjas get more Western while our cowboys get more Ninjified. Well, that's love, or capitalism: you appropriate the strange and then sell it back modified.

Fishin'

My father took me fishing once. He marched me to the riverbank and snapped a picture of me with a fishing rod in my hand, then we went home. Consequently, I've never seen the point. My friend Keith's father took *him* fishing, too. "He just screamed and hollered at me!" Keith said, but they always caught a lot of fish. Consequently, Keith sees the point. He goes fishing, and the other day he took me and my son with him. My son thinks a father and son should go fishing too, because that's what he picked up somewhere, probably from Andy Griffith.

We fish. It's a beautiful day on Lake Borgne, which empties into the Gulf of Mexico. We've been launched into the water in Keith's motorboat with a bucket full of live shrimp and two bags of ice by an old geezer whose shack is bumperstickered PATROLLED BY SMITH & WESSON and FIGHT ORGANIZED CRIME: ABOLISH THE IRS. The calm lake pacifies me almost at once. In the distance there are shrimpers on their way to the Gulf. We stay near the mouths of the bayous where the trout are.

I've never caught a fish in my life and I don't care if I do, but there is a tug on my line. To the enthusiastic shouts of my son, I reel in a speckled trout. Just as I do this, Keith's rod jumps violently. He reels hard, and there...there is a shark on his hook. It's about three feet long, and it looks exactly like its cousin in *Jaws*. We net it with some difficulty and stuff it in the ice chest: it thrashes powerfully in there. My son is now completely transported, particularly when, almost immediately after it's cast, Keith's line is pulled taut by a *second* shark. This one fights harder, snaps the line, and is gone with the hook in its mouth.

And so it goes—no more shark, but we pull in trout after trout, a real orgy of plenty and luck and excitement. I feel momentarily something like regret about never having fished with my father. My son is confirmed in his new faith. Keith's father looms behind all this, an archetypal Fisher Father setting in motion all the sons of the world. The sun burns brilliantly over the marsh grass full of red-winged blackbirds.

I don't even have a camera.

Surrogate Mom

We live in the age of surrogates but we may be running up against the limits of it. We put up with substitutions of all kinds, and have been made progressively more tolerant of the loss of the genuine. The forces of the fake are now testing the last frontier: the human body. Television's bionic man, woman, and dog have prepared us for the advent of people made largely out of machine parts.

That sort of preparation was not, it seems, enough for Mary Beth Whitehead, the "surrogate mom" in New Jersey who decided to keep the baby she carried and gave birth to. Although the fertilized egg belonged to others, Mary Beth refused to see herself as a surrogate. After nine months of making a new human and giving birth to it, she decided that she was the genuine article after all, not merely an incubating machine for a rich couple's egg. Mary Beth's act is a class revolt. She has said no to the power of money to turn a human being into a thing. "I only signed on an egg, I never signed on the life of a child," she said. Indeed. Surrogate motherhood is a novel form of exploitation, one that aims to establish a new view of the human body as simply a container, a repository of organs. Imitation and simulation have now been in the world long enough to feel that they are in fact reality, which is why the human body is their next target. No human beings in history, no matter how exploited, have ever considered themselves surrogates, imitation humans, simulated creatures performing only mechanical functions. In the worst cases, they have been killed as being part of someone bigger, a king for instance, but it was as humans that they were disposed of.

A philosophical shift does not occur when a machine says, "I'm a human being." It does occur when a human being says, "I'm a machine." Mary Beth has drawn a battle line. Kudos for her. It will be a long battle, regardless of the outcome of her case. In the end, I suspect, the human cause will be lost. That day, look for a new kind of store at your shopping mall.

Vanishing Children

M y wife's cousin called my wife to ask how she was doing. "I'm getting a certificate to teach art to children," Alice told her. There was a small, disappointed *oh!* on the other end. Alice, you see, is a painter. Her cousin has an exalted idea of artists as doomed and lonely creatures and, to her, teaching doesn't sound so romantic. Had Alice said, "I'm running away from home to a freezing loft in Paris," her cousin would have been breathless with excitement. She would have been equally excited if Alice had announced that she was going to law school. But teaching? Teaching *children*? That just seems like drudgery.

Women everywhere nowadays leave their children in the care of others while they pursue careers. Children just aren't *in*, although having them certainly is. But once they're had, and proudly displayed alongside the CD player, the Volvo, and the sailboat, it's time to hand them over to someone else. Only the poor are stuck with their own children. If you can afford to, you hand your kids to the poor. First they baby-sit, then they educate them—that is, if you can still find them. Statistic after statistic shows an alarming drop in the number of people interested in teaching, especially at the earlier levels. Children, bad enough at home, must be truly horrible *en masse*.

Starving artists, lawyers, fashion models, and bartenders have more in common with each other than they do with teachers. The new class distinctions are between people stuck with children and people who've managed to get away from them. Teachers, like social workers and nuns, are throwbacks to the ancient liberal past, a quaint minority without a trace of chic. The new American lower class is the socially conscious. Fashion, not money, defines the new hierarchies.

There is a lovely and sad poem by Lawrence Ferlinghetti

about a man driving around in a car with five changes of clothes for his different lifestyles, who cannot remember where his children are. They "dropped out," the poet says, "into Nothing / in a Jungian search / for lost parents / their own age." There is nothing in our society helpful to raising children who can in turn raise children. Glamour attaches to the maintenance of one's eternal adolescence, which is only commercialized childhood, a limbo state where one is neither child nor grown-up but Perpetual Consumer.

The real children, meanwhile, vanish like the rest of the unfashionable world, through the wrong side of the TV glass.

Vagaries of Pseudo-Fame

I'm pseudo-famous. I was conversing with a friend on the Greyhound, when the lady in front of us whipped around in her seat and said, "*I know your voice!*" "Well, sure," I said, trying to remember whether the conversation I was having contained any embarrassing parts. It's bad enough when somebody recognizes your face from someplace. You get a second of *aha*! about that person's eyes. You can take half of it to understand that you've been recognized, and you can use the other half to turn yourself into something social. But there is no warning if that same somebody recognizes your voice. He's upon you before you can pull in your horns, or pull up your shades, as the case may be.

A few years ago, a Romanian friend and I were riding the subway in New York City, speaking our native language loudly and delighting in the public pronouncing of certain filthy expressions. All was going well with the uncomprehending natives, who knew not what taboos we were smashing, until an elderly and distinguished gentleman seated right in front of us turned and, in the most crystalline Romanian, said, "You should be ashamed of yourselves!" We were, believe me. Since then I've been leery of public displays of intimate vocabulary, Romanian *or* English. And since the time I began performing on radio, I've been leery of public displays of my *voice*. What does it matter if strangers overhear a friendly conversation, provided, of course, that it isn't intended to shock or even reach their ears? Well, a stranger who knows your voice isn't a stranger: he's a listener.

The lady on the bus was a nice person. She said the nice things people say on such occasions. The friend with whom I'd been talking said, "You're famous." "Sure," I said, and turned to the guy behind me, a student going home for the weekend.

"Do I know you from somewhere?" I asked.

"Maybe," he said. "I hang out at the Union."

"You're pretty famous," I said.

"Not like Henry Kissinger or anything," quoth he.

Death Dreams

E very few years I have a powerful dream about death. Last night I died in a burst of gunfire from someone I like a lot. I asked him why he killed me. "Because you're famous," he said. That seemed reasonable enough, and after I died, I continued to ponder the question of reasonableness. Being dead was the same as being alive, only I didn't have a body and people didn't see me. Nevertheless, I continued to influence the living through a channel called "the crystal passage." Things were so ordinary that I even read my obituaries in the newspapers and noted that they made excessive use of the phrase "full of life." But now I was dead. And felt just the same.

My last dream on the subject had been ecstatic and colorful. Dying was a liberating experience, and although still intensely interested in human affairs immediately after croaking, I gradually came to take no notice of them and at last dissolved into the shimmering fabric of sheer joy. I even noted that death is "negative copying" while birth is "positive copying," a sort of Xerox process that reproduces DNA in two opposite directions.

Ten years have passed between the one dream and the other, and the difference seems to be that the world has gained greater weight in me. I mean, it would never have occurred to me ten years ago to read my obituaries. I was in too great a hurry then to get to the fun stuff, the cosmic light show. Ten years ago I thought nothing of leaving the human dialogue unfinished, in mid-sentence, and going off to play with something else. Now, it seems, I'd like to keep talking as if there were somewhere to get to that way.

Nonetheless, last night's dream was a liberating one. There is an Indian legend in which Satan makes a body and tricks an angel into momentarily inhabiting it. The angel does and then Satan won't let him out. But after living in this body for a few years, the angel discovers that a powerful goddess also lives in there with him. It is Death, and she can let him out any time he wants to go. It was a nice discovery. It came to him in a dream.

To Disappear

Have you ever wanted to disappear? Pick up one day and go, and never come back? Your family would miss you, look for you, feel terrible, but, after a time, what could they do? They'd give up. Your friends would remember you every time they got drunk. They would remember only good things: you would grow less and less flawed in their memory until you became a myth.

Where would you disappear to? Well, it's a big country. There are thousands of little towns, dozens of big cities. You could work in a gas station where nobody asks questions. The other fellows working there would probably be dropouts from some other life, too. Every year, thousands of people vanish. They haven't been murdered; they've just grown sick of how they live. They're sick of responsibilities, of social obligations. They're bored to tears. Some are intellectuals sick of ideas, who'd now like to work quietly with their hands. Some are in flight from the middle class, sick of shopping, debts, insurance, bosses, planning for the future. Some are just plain tired of talking, or of keeping on a good face despite a sinking feeling.

I once lived in a town where fewer than half the people used the names they were born with. Some were fugitives from justice; others were just dropouts from the rat race. The town had no mayor, no officials, no police. It got wild at times but everyone seemed to know how to take care of themselves. One guy I knew had been a corporate bigwig in Boston. Now he did carpentry on and off. "I used to feel helpless then," he said. "Now I just take things as they come."

Not everyone in town was nouveau poor or downwardly

mobile. Some had disappeared because they just couldn't stand people. That was OK, too. People left them alone.

Of course, you could always disappear right where you are now, like that guy in the Hawthorne story did: take a room across the street from your family, watch your wife get remarried, your kids grow old. But that's another story.

The Price of Dreams

T he other day when the stock market crashed, I took inven-
tory of my dreams. Some of them are now worth about half
what they were when I first had them, while others are easily
worth five times as much.

Real dreams, the ones I dream at night, have appreciated
greatly. I have kept a dream diary for twenty years. As I page
through the black bound notebooks I find interesting pictures of
the future which, all but invisible to me during waking hours, is
in fact clearly outlined in the night. There is, for instance, this
picture from a decade ago of a powerful gray horse on top of
which I am swimming the waters of a great bright lake. Lured by
the sight of a beautiful island castle, we stop for a rest. My horse
is taken to a stable while I am brought before a great fireplace
where I am feasted and pampered by beautiful maidens until I
fall asleep. At some point during the night within the night of
my sleep within sleep, I wake up troubled and scared. "Bring me
my horse!" I shout. Too well fed and drowsy, I clamber aboard
my somewhat fatter and slower steed and regain the great water
which is now gray, menacing and indefinite, unlike the brilliant,
sparkling body of before. Still, there is a sense that all is not lost,
although I am a little confused and my future is uncertain. I
deduce from this dream that I should never settle for the lure of
too-easy comfort but should, instead, stay in the current of actual
events. No hiding in ivory castles. My life has borne me out
these past ten years. Whenever something looks too good to pass
up, I trot out this great steed of a dream and am renewed.

Unlike the dreams of the night, which cannot but increase in
value if properly considered, my daydreams have not fared very
well. This may be because they are merely wishes born of greed

instead of harsh unconscious images. One daydream in particular has fared worse and worse while getting stronger and stronger. Whenever I am exhausted or merely wistful I like to imagine myself floating in a small boat on a blue lake with mountains all around it. When I first had this dream I was young and didn't have a job and I could get to a mountain lake in half a day. Today, ten years later, I work in the swamps and the mountains are far away. Ten years ago I thought this a pleasing fantasy. I now think it an intensely wonderful one. As the price of actualizing my dream doubled, I added a dream house to the dream lake and in it I installed a huge dream tub with a picture window overlooking this lake and mountains. My dream has now quadrupled in both desirability and value and so has my inability to get there soon. As I realize that I may never get to that lake, I become very afraid. To keep that fear at bay I dream harder, adding a bigger boat, a bluer lake, a deeper tub, a wider window. My dream greed keeps my very real fear from ever telling me the truth, which is that the greedier I get the farther away the dream gets from its realization. What began in simple fantasy has become an excuse for not seeing the truth, and when the fantasy at last becomes too ridiculous, it will burst. The fear that will follow will be, I know, the cold light of truth.

The wise men of the market tell us that its main drive is greed. They tell us that everything is all right, that the fear it now reveals is only temporary, that greed will soon return. Oh, greed, we miss you terribly!

Insofar as the market is the great tissue of everyone's daydreams of riches, it does echo my small daydream in a way. Aristotle says that drama is driven by two main emotions, fear and pity. That was true for a while, at least for as long as writers believed it, but then like other things Aristotelian, that scheme fell apart and new emotions showed up, embarrassment among them. If the market were more like literature, it wouldn't have crashed: pity is a fine counter to fear, and embarrassment a good humble antidote to all things human. But the market isn't literature and it certainly isn't human. Pity is what the greedy would like us to feel for them now that they are seized by fear. But what we feel instead is embarrassment. We reserve pity for our own daydreams, which resemble the fallen market more than they should. Meanwhile, we would do better to listen to what the night has to tell us in the language of the unconscious. Real dreams never depreciate.

Scars

Y ears ago, Sherrill Jaffee wrote a book called *Scars Make the Body More Beautiful*, an aesthetic proposition that still very much intrigues me. I'm pretty smooth myself, except for a scar between thumb and forefinger incurred in a knife fight when I was ten. There was much blood and mothers screaming at each other, and my opponent ended up with a nice gash too that later turned into a beautiful scar on his chin. I have also an almost indistinguishable mark on my forehead caused by a telephone pole the first time I got drunk. It had been my first date as well, and I took the incident as a warning against combining such potent intoxicants as love and alcohol.

Most other people are pretty banged-up, however, and will point with great delight to the commemorative marks of the body's battle with the material world. "I got this falling off a horse," someone will say, tracing the long thin crescent on his cheek. "This one's from falling off a skateboard," says someone else, pointing to a knee. Men love their football injuries and women love their appendectomy and cesarean scars. And their lovers, they hope, do too. When they do not, it usually means that love is at an end. The test of true love is the pleasure one takes in the scars of one's beloved.

Most scars, it seems, are from falling, others from cutting, but wherever they come from they do make the body more interesting if not more beautiful. We don't practice ritual scarification here in New Orleans, but there are plenty of us tattooed discreetly or not so discreetly. Tattoos are, however, too deliberate for my taste. A butterfly drawn above an ankle or a multicolored dragon on a back are startling apparitions. But do they inspire passion? Sublime art *can* inspire passion, but sublimity is rarely found in tattoos. Most of them are the work of fairground hacks, hardly the stuff to send one soaring. Sure, a bold tattoo enables one to recognize another person quickly if one has no memory for names or faces. On the Greyhound I often hear people refer to "the dude with the heart on his cheek" or "the chick with the cross on her forehead." Most of us, luckily, don't need such flags to remember—or to be remembered.

It is the accidental scar that tells the human story: it redraws the map of the body by becoming the center of events; the surrounding skin points to the scar the way wilderness draws around a city. There is no science of scar reading like those of palm and forehead reading, but there should be—it would make so much more sense. Scars are a good map of one's past. Old soldiers could probably tell history by their wounds. They ought to teach it to children by displaying their scars: "This one's from Normandy, boys. . . ." Scars are the signatures of healing and they ought to be displayed proudly as triumphs over infection and war.

By mapping the past, scars can also tell the future. Marks that the body acquires on its journey define its future better than those it was born with and had no say over. Why should the predetermined lines in one's palm tell the story of a being whose circumstances and life are subject to constant change? And how can these predetermined lines tell what's in a person's heart, what wounds he or she has sustained?

The other day, my friends and I spent much time after dinner discussing our scars. The human race is well scarred, if my friends are any indication. Not one of them is without a blemish, praise the fates.

We have lived—and there are traces.

Let's Twist Again

Dance: the mystery of motion. "He who does not dance, neither shall he eat," said Tuli Kupferberg in an addendum to the Ten Commandments. Tuli sings and dances. I sometimes sing (when nobody's within earshot) and dance (when I've had enough drinks to forget myself). But I prefer to watch dancers, until, as Yeats said, I cannot tell "the dancer from the dance." The fact is that the universe itself is a dance, and its elements move to music.

I recently saw *Hairspray*, John Waters's delightful homage to the early 1960s, the age of a thousand new dances. People in the sixties, possessed by uncanny energy, began to boogie across the country as if it were the polished surface of a giant mirror. Every day, a new dance. The energy it took to dance them was the same energy, no doubt, that put Americans on the moon. Space was the dominant metaphor of the age. We pointed our rockets at the sky, we drove our fin-tailed cars across the continent, we questioned the division of our country by race and color, we believed that we could be anywhere and everywhere at once. And what's more, we felt the *rightness* of moving, its savage truth. And move we did, oola-boola, boogie-woogie, twist 'n' shout, rock 'n' roll.

In retrospect, you can define any period in light of its dominant dance. Ages move as people do. The Edwardian age waltzed off the deck of the *Titanic* into oblivion. The twenties and the thirties fox-trotted and jitter-bugged their way into the War, and came out battered at the other end in the frenzied intensity of conga lines and communal victory dances. Our dances, worldly as they are, don't differ much from the sacred dances of natives in India, Africa, or Mexico. When we dance we become possessed by both personal demons and gods. Most of these demons and gods are ancient, but one of them is always new: the god (or demon) of the age we live in, the spirit of the times.

So then, what kind of age is this? I went to The Ritz, a New York nightclub, to watch the latest moves. An agitated crowd in black leather jumped up and down in the same place as if everyone was desperately trying to pull up roots but could not. Now and again a desperate person would climb up on stage and throw himself off, falling seven feet into the arms of his generation. Miraculously, they caught him before he broke his neck. It was an act of supreme faith, confirmed, if not by compassion, then surely by the density and immobility of the crowd. The music was loud, repetitious, bleak, insistent, raw.

Punk isn't, of course, the dominant dance style of our time, but it's the most visibly different. Perhaps there is no dominant dance now. People don't seem to dance any special new dance: if they don't just sway to the music or jump up and down, they do old dances in ritual or even archival ways. Nobody is inventing steps. It's a sad thing, really, reminiscent of the situation of apples. Once there were hundreds of varieties of apples in this country. Now there are only two: the A&P apple and the Safeway apple. Punk and museum. Desperation and nostalgia.

In Transylvania, where I grew up, we had lots of kinds of apples but only two dances: the waltz and the folk. Folk dancing was actually a whole lot of different dances but to an adolescent it was just one dance: embarrassing. Our parents waltzed, but we didn't care about that. Then a miracle occurred: the spirit of the times slipped through the Iron Curtain. The first new dance to slip through was the Twist, and we all started to twist with a vengeance. It was more than a dance, it was a political stance. We twisted against the government, the official radio, school, borders, boredom, and phony nationalism. We twisted internationally, hoping to merge with our generation all over the world. I, for one, twisted right out of the country. Alas, it's still the only dance I can do.

When I got to the United States in 1966, people weren't doing steps anymore, they were swaying to internal rhythms. Music had become self-reflexive, self-conscious, and introspective, just like the divided Vietnam generation. One could do whatever one wanted on the floor, but it was a formless possession. Things got moving again in the seventies with the mindless disco beat, but I never acquired a taste for it. Today, after the required drinks, I'll twist. In any case, if by their dances you shall know them, our age will be known as The Age of the Swaying Muddle, the time when some swayed, while most just milled around.

In the fifties we got far enough off the ground to get to outer space, while in the eighties we barely have enough energy to jump up and down on the small piece of turf under our feet. Maybe the spirit of our times is only a collage of the spirits of other times, and the most we can get out of it is Instant Replay. Perish the thought. A time without an original Dance God is a lost time. I believe that whatever is nailing our feet to the floor now ought to lift us up again. "Times might be a-changing'," as Divine says in *Hairspray*. After all, the signs are everywhere: the recent spate of UFO sightings, the glimpses of Elvis's ghost . . .

But then it may just be the year 1963 making its fourth or fifth attempt at a comeback.

Imitationi Mediae

My friend Pat Nolan says that life, which used to imitate art, now imitates *The National Enquirer*. The key to scandal in English-speaking countries has always been "Find the money!" but now we've also taken up the cry of the French, which has always been "Cherchez la femme!" Does this mean that British stolidity is about to be replaced by French frivolity? Are we learning at last to have fun?

I don't think so. The sex hysteria spreading through the nation like the blush over the cheek of a shocked monk is a virus from outer space. It corresponds neither to the prevailing weather of current feelings about sex nor to so-called community standards. Prevailing weather is anything if not steamy. Cable television, from Dr. Ruth to MTV, is spreading sexual ideas from sea to shining sea, reaching even those places where you can still get slapped across the face by your mom for saying the word *sex*. Condoms and what to do with them are on everyone's mind. (It seems kind of hard to separate them from what they are for.) Community standards, which used to exist when this country had a variety of communities, are all the same now that we've become one community: TV viewers. We all live on TV now, between Dallas and Anywhere or Nowhere. The TV community worshiped the purity of Vanna White, the goddess of meaning, until she appeared scantily clad in *Playboy*. Then other, less virginal goddesses had their turn: Donna Rice, Jessica Hahn, and Debra Murphree, who should, as Jerry Hunt suggests, get together to form a musical group singing old Martha and the Vandellas tunes.

So between steamy weather and TV-inspired community standards, where does the outrage at old-fashioned "sex scandal" come from? Polls show that the public wasn't scandalized by Gary Hart; it felt vaguely sympathetic for him. One can only conclude that the current sex-scandal mania is just one more aspect of the generalized sex mania in this country, and that the public, which, after all, lives on TV, actually feels neither outrage nor amazement for the phenomena because it is too busy viewing itself to feel a strong emotion. This narcissistic absorption corresponds neither to reality nor to desire, which lie unexpressed. The public opinion survey, which reflects only this self-reflection, further enforces the silence. Public sex is to real sex what the opinion poll is to true feeling. When we believe that the opinion polls represent us we lose our selves. Likewise, we are about to cede the singular expression of our sexuality to its pornographic symbols.

Smut Now

U pon receiving the latest issue of my magazine, *Exquisite Corpse*, my mother tore it up, then called to tell me about it.

"I tore your rag to ribbons!" she exclaimed.

"Why?" I asked, innocently pursuing what I've known to be, since my earliest childhood, a futile question.

"Smut!" pronounced Mother. And then, so as there be no trace of doubt, she added, "Let literature be literature and smut *smut!*"

I was stunned where I stood, receiver in hand. I edit a rather classy rag, if I may say so myself. There are articles in it about Wittgenstein and Friedrich Nietzsche, for Chrissakes.

At long last, after many pregnant pauses, I ascertained what had bugged Mother. On page six there was a little story about a horny couple romping in a graveyard. I tried explaining, but it was an uphill battle. My mother, unfortunately, was not the Supreme Court of the 1960s, which knocked down the definition of porn to make room for Henry Miller, William Burroughs, and Allen Ginsberg. Do you think that today's Supreme Court would have been so perceptive? I doubt it, especially in light of the following astonishing anecdote.

The other day, at a New York restaurant, at a banquet in honor of William Burroughs, author of *Junky* and *Queer*, Allen Ginsberg lectured a friend of mine against overusing the F-word. My friend was using this word mostly as an adjective, the way it's come down through the decades and the way it is commonly used most everywhere where people talk normally. I mean, there was Allen Ginsberg, in a suit and tie, over a plate of lobster, telling my friend that his anger wasn't *cool*. Allen G., who wrote "Howl." That poem can be found today in *The Norton Anthology*, for any freshman to learn.

So what does it all mean? It means that the tone of our times is different from the "Sixties," and that Allen Ginsberg, no less than my mother, is reflecting it. Personally, I think that the almost complete disappearance of that word from print, if not from life, dreadfully impoverishes the erotic-political pool of the nation.

Write a letter to the editor, Mom.

Theory F

I can solve the budget deficit. It's very simple, really. Every time you say the F-word, put five cents in a can. At the end of the year, turn it over to the government. If there is still a deficit next year, I'll eat my F-ing hat.

There are two schools of thought about the present state of our language: one says that English is growing, the other that it's shrinking. Those who think it's growing simply point to the fact that we are constantly coining new words. Those who think it's shrinking cite the rise of minimal slang, headed by the F-word. William Arrowsmith, a classics scholar, reviewed the second unabridged edition of *The Random House Dictionary* and noted with disgust the vast number of slang words sanctioned there. Yes, there were *more* words, he admitted, but they shouldn't be allowed in the book, for they go in at the expense of *good* words. QED, the language is shrinking.

The shrink-partisans are conservatives, the growth-fanciers liberals. Both conservatives and liberals bemoan the enormity of the budget deficit. I propose a compromise: for every personal use of a controversial word—particularly the F-word and its variations—put five cents in the can. Conservatives would put in their five cents for doing something that shouldn't be allowed, and liberals would put in theirs because they're glad it's allowed. Everybody would be happy, and the deficit would disappear.

Not so long ago, parents washed out their children's mouths with soap whenever they swore. Now parents can take it out of their kids' allowance. And a big kid like Eddie Murphy, for instance, who has never spoken a whole sentence without using the F-word five or six times, would contribute quite a deal. From each according to his needs.

Everyone knows how much our men in power curse. It has something to do with the headiness of authority. If Nixon had paid for all his expletives, the budget deficit would now be considerably smaller. Here in Louisiana the politicians could wipe out our state deficit in a month—the big guns in Baton Rouge just *love* to talk dirty.

Five cents on each use is not a bad tax, and what's even better about it is that it's a *private* tax. Nobody'll need to enforce it: it's just between you and how you feel about your country. It's not an ideological tax. It's a cheap way to feel patriotic.

The Perfect Crime

Here at the *Exquisite Corpse* office we have tightened security considerably ever since it occurred to us that we could be the victims of the perfect crime. Suppose that somebody's got it in for us, maybe one of those fanatical outfits that calls itself the World Academic Freedom Something–or–other, but which is in reality a cover for some Victorian poetry society, which is itself a cover for all the poets whose work we've rejected. Rejection, let's face it, is not easy to take. Look what Hitler did just because people didn't like his paintings. So this World Academic Freedom Council-or-something decides to become the scourge of unrhymed poetry by eliminating some of the editors who publish it. Unrhymed poetry is synonymous in some circles with communism, atheism, anarchism, radicalism, obscenity, and the breakdown of society at all levels. I don't say they are wrong: if blame must be found, it might as well be found in unbound verse. But instead of letting congressmen, chancellors, department chairmen, fire chiefs, city aldermen, and sewage and police commissioners know about it, these Freedom people decide to commit the perfect crime instead.

Every day here at the *Exquisite Corpse* office there are hundreds of envelopes to be licked. Every poet sends us an S.A.S.E., or self-addressed stamped envelope, with his or her submission so that we can return the material should we reject it. Since the only use of an S.A.S.E. is rejection, you can imagine the temptation of a frustrated poet—particularly a Victorian, raised on Sherlock Holmes—to take revenge *ahead of time* for an assumed rejection. A drop of cyanide on the glue of the return envelope and *bingo*! revenge is served. And it's the perfect crime, since the evidence is mailed back to the murderer and so ceases to exist. This is why we have decided to hire somebody to lick self-addressed stamped envelopes. Safe editing makes good sense these days. The perfect crime is waiting for the righteous.

Sodomy

E ver since the recent Supreme Court ruling on sodomy, I've been noticing it everywhere. I went to a museum: nothing but sodomy on the walls. The ancient pottery depicted nothing but sodomy, and everybody in history used to drink from that stuff. Of course, I thought: art is the work of sodomites, and everybody influenced by art is a sodomite too. I looked up at the thousands of windows of my city. All those people in all those rooms, all alone with their art and their sodomy.

Books, too, are full of sodomy. You can barely bump into a story these days without some sodomites right smack in the middle of it. Not that the old stories are better: they are full of unresolved sodomite tension. It is better not to read, but then one might bump into folk tales and myths, which, as everyone knows, are nothing but one sodomy after another. People in them sodomize sheep. Even in jokes people sodomize pigs. The movies, God knows, aren't any better: the sodomites of Hollywood have managed to push their ideas into every picture you see. Even so-called family entertainment is probably full of subliminal sodomy. Who knows what lies hidden in "Lassie" and *Bambi*?

Clearly, history, art, literature, joke telling, and the cinema are agents of sodomy. Everyone they touch is liable to go home and practice. The Supreme Court didn't go far enough: it should have hit the plague at its roots by enjoining us from history and art. But that really isn't my concern. You see, Americans are stubborn people. They don't like to be told what not to do. I fear that sodomy will now spread. People who until now have been content with the missionary position after a hard day in church might take up sodomy just out of spite. And protest groups, helped by rock 'n' roll, which is nothing but musical sodomy, may take up the cause.

Instead of Hands Across America . . .

AIDS and the Tired Man

R e-lax-a-tion, mind you, does not come easily in these days of nervous prosperity, so it was with some pleasure and a feeling of infinite lassitude that I sank into my favorite divan with the latest *Time* and Dr. Ruth on TV. I'd been caught up in writing a book and hadn't been noticing what the country was up to. Last time I'd left it, children were being molested and there was cyanide in the aspirin. "My boyfriend's penis," a woman said, "is too big." "Does he lubricate you enough?" asked Dr. Ruth. "If you do not wear a condom, you're going to die," said *Time* magazine. Poor woman! With a condom on it, her boyfriend's penis would be even bigger. "And many condoms," warned *Time*, "just aren't thick enough." Something the consistency of galoshes would probably do.

In the future, I sighed to myself, relaxing more and more, only the Michelin man will be allowed to have sex. It's the common man who's mucked it all up again. AIDS is nothing but democracy in action. In the old days only poets and aristocrats were allowed to have sex and fun at the same time. The masses were forbidden to confuse procreation with recreation. Now look at the mess! First the vote, now the plague! "Dr. Ruth," another woman said, "I can only have an orgasm in the shower. My boyfriend doesn't help at all!" "It's everybody you've been with the past five years," said *Time* magazine. I flipped the page and there was an ad for instant coffee. Five years in the age of instant coffee! Very interesting! What will now happen to instant coffee, the microwave oven, the frozen dinner, and fast food if party sex is out? The only reason for instant anything is to make time for sex in this world where everybody's either working, in school, in prison, or in the army. Now we'll have to throw away our throwaway society and wear rubber from head to toe. "Dr. Ruth, I have a nightmare every night that I'm wearing a condom on my head and can't get it off!" "Grasp the condom firmly," said *Time*, "and yank it out resolutely!"

Indeed. And then put on some New Age music and forget about everything.

Nouvelle Erogeny

Flossing and kissing can give you AIDS. This sad fact, one among many, from my morning paper. Actually, any wet contact between humans can spread the virus. Animals were not included in the report—but since monkeys have AIDS too, it might be cautious to include your pets in the general injunction. No more tongue-kissing your cat.

Clearly, our erogeny needs rethinking. Instead of wet-to-wet contact we must make wet-to-dry contact and vice versa. The skin is a very good prophylactic except in places where it leaks and these should be sealed shut with latex. (Eyeglasses are also an excellent prophylactic. I have been using mine for years to keep my eyes from making reality pregnant.) Perhaps all the seven openings of the body should be surgically removed to a single area, the top of the head, let's say. That would make it possible for a good hat to cover all the mischief.

Another suggestion, made by a dedicated reactionary, is that we give in to our true nature, which is masturbatory. Sex is an invention of the media: no one really wants to do it, but it's hard not to when you read in the paper about all the sex everyone's having. If we didn't have to keep up with the Joneses, we could all do what we'd like to do best anyway: go back to the fifties. The music was better then, and we had patriotism. And we masturbated on the slightest pretext, to the bra ads in the *New York Times*. With all of one's openings clustered at the top of the head under a hat, it would be easy to masturbate by just nodding in time to fifties bop. This way we could save the world and still have fun.

I'm not suggesting implementing all of this at once. We might begin by drying up a little every day, and visualizing the new body, and the nouvelle erogeny which, like nouvelle cuisine, is mainly in the mind.

Indecent Exposure

A young woman flings open her overcoat. She is wearing only the merest bikini. The crowd cheers. As she begins to peel it off to rhythmic applause, a mounted policeman whips through the citizenry and lifts her brusquely onto his steed. She flashes the "V" sign to the crowd from behind the massive blue back. On the counter of a bar, two naked men dance with each other, and a crowd piles through the doorway to watch. A man dangles some cheap beads from a balcony and a girl below flashes her chest. Under the next balcony, a goggle of revelers is enticing a pair of amply endowed middle-aged women to "show your tits!", which they do, once the enticement becomes sufficiently musical and seductive. Breasts are bared, bottoms revealed, and genitals flaunted, but only when beads are offered or when the music and applause achieve a certain pitch, and not a moment before.

It is carnival time in New Orleans, and a good percentage of the population is doing what it likes to do best: expose itself. Despite the dangers of sporadic law enforcement, indecent exposure is sweeping the French Quarter like a bush . . . er, brush fire. It isn't just freaks, either. Folks so respectable that at home they are probably presidents of banks and heads of the PTA are taking their pleasure in anonymous transgression. It's one of the charms of Mardi Gras that mild Dionysian rites are tolerated, but the rites themselves are a sign that we Americans are desperately repressed.

We are a nation of TV watchers with an insatiable appetite for voyeurism and exposure. We watch movie and TV stars continually tease us with selected patches of their flesh showing through carefully designed gaps. The very fabric of the mass media is itself designed to show provocative folds, daring seams, and sudden partings of materials. If one looked entirely between the lines of a television entertainment, one would find that the composition consists entirely of rifts, cracks, seemingly inadvertent openings, rips, tears, and oblique views. The real action in most entertainment is in the interstices. Our own actions in regard to these entertainments are usually passive, purely voyeuristic. Sometimes we do get up in the middle of the night to adjust the satellite dish to better pick up the teasing seams of space, but most of the time we just lie there. Then carnival comes, and suddenly, through carefully concealed gaps in our business suits and modest shifts, the flesh presses irrepressibly forth.

Love and Croissants

I t's worth getting out of bed some mornings. And it's a pleasure, especially if the pale winter sun is out and shining, to delight with your lover in the urban gift of your favorite café. Fresh coffee, steaming croissants, and the Sunday papers. Ah! All the way to ours, Alice and I talked about love and how many people don't get any while others get a lot, and how that unfairness probably accounts for the federal deficit and crooked contracting practices, and so on. The café was crowded but a friend of ours, who was sitting with two other people, waved and we joined them.

The two people were pleasant-looking folks in their thirties, a man and a woman who looked well married to me. "I don't know these people," our friend Chris said, "I just joined them."

"That's all right," said the man, "I don't know the lady, either, We're on a blind date."

We turned to face her, and she blushed. "Yeah," she said. "We met through the personals."

"Amazing," said Chris, "I've talked to the both of you longer than you have to each other!"

It turns out that they'd met not just through a personal ad but through a personal ad in the local gay paper which neither one of them reads but which their best friends do.

"What did you say about yourself?" asked Alice.

"Oh," he said, without much hesitation, "'Mr. Congeniality and Jimmy Connors lookalike seeks soul mate with body to match.'"

"What did you answer?" I asked the woman.

Before she could reply, her date answered for her: "She went on about how intelligent she was! And how she likes to talk!"

The woman drew herself in slightly as he spoke for her. And

then she looked him over carefully, and smiled. He was no Jimmy Connors lookalike, that's for sure. Maybe once, but not any longer. And he looked back, like a kid who'd been caught, and he smiled too, as something passed between them.

It wasn't our business anymore, but as the pale winter sun flooded the crowded café, I thought that these two might have a chance. They had not, it is true, talked privately yet, but they had taken more risks than people who meet in the "normal" (whatever that is) way. In any case, here was their answer. Difficult, yes. Possible, certainly. Interesting, always.

The Woes of Translation

The heat descends on New Orleans these days like an invisible parachute, and I am wrestling the angel of translation. Is that *my* sentence? If it sounds odd to me it's because I'm suspended between two languages like someone whose parachute has caught on two trees.

I am translating from the Romanian the favorite poet of my youth, Lucian Blaga. He is a poet of mists and shadows, old medieval towers, and haunted piazzas. His best poems were written just before World War II and there is a prophetic rumble in them of the tanks and planes and horrible suffering to come. How render that sound into American, I ask you? How put those melancholy undertones of a world soon to die into the splashy vowels of a decade of screen blips and holistic health? Were it not for my translingual belief that madness is just as much present here and now as it was in Romania then, I would probably give up.

But I won't. In fact, much as translation of any kind seems impossible, I still believe in it. Translation is itself transcendent. I was once a Romanian and I translated myself into an American. I wake up in the morning and translate myself from a dreamer into a typist. Night translates into day, everybody translates subtly or crudely from the people they were one minute to the people they are going to be the next. Translation isn't just an operation of language, it's the way every living thing makes itself known to another. We come into each others' presence through countless acts of translation. Our troubles come from endlessly misreading these translations. Greeks shake their heads from left to right to mean yes, up and down to mean no. Bodies, like languages, are often shipwrecked on the shoals of shabby translation. We learn each other like children learning to read, continuously translating how we feel into what we know. Unconsciousness translates into consciousness precisely as languages do, because they *are* languages. *Traduttore/tradittore:* translator/traitor, says the old saw, and often it is true. In spite of it we somehow make ourselves understood, even loved.

Well then, old poet, should we negotiate that narrow rope-bridge of consonants between two eras, hoping it will hold us?

It should hold, like the heat.

Running

I've been running. Not *from* anything, mind you. Not *toward* anything either. Just running, like millions of other Americans who don't care how silly they look. As recently as two weeks ago I said, and I am quoting myself, "I will never run." I was not playing the coy politician, and I was not merely running off at the mouth. I was expressing a deep-seated belief that all motion should be useful and directed toward an immediate goal.

People who make empty, automatic gestures like crossing their eyes over and over, or violently jerking their heads to the right, have always looked crazy to me. In some sense, however, people who do such things are less silly than runners. Tics are a kind of kinetic geometry by means of which a person sets right certain things in his immediate world. Or, if crazy enough, the whole world. I have a friend who thinks that if he does not shrug his shoulders three times while rubbing his forehead with the index finger of his right hand, his family and his nation-state will suffer a horrible fate. Running always appeared to me as something of that order: a collective tic by means of which we exorcise the nameless dread that haunts our consumer society.

A number of my friends say they run for their health, but that doesn't seem a very convincing reason to me. "Health," like "destiny" or "welfare," is an abstract notion that has little to do with human beings living in the real world. "That person's health is good" means only that that person is not likely to die in the doctor's office. As soon as he steps out—Look out, here comes that bus! Or that proverbial brick! No, the idea of "good health" is nothing but a tic of the mind.

Another thing I hold against running is that runners get mean after they run for a while. That's a fact they talk about often in the running magazines, and if you look at a runner's contorted face, with that peculiar crossing of pain and grim determination on it, you can see what they mean. There are exceptions, of course. Like that girl in the latest two-tone running shorts, the one with the flying hair who just went by in a whoosh of scented, warm air that I hasten to inhale. She may have been Florence Griffith Joyner, trailing the love of the nation behind her. I can't be sure, she was too fast.

I am running. It's a drug. It's a bird, a plane . . . I am high, I sweat, I soar above the peasants, I dispense euphoria. I can't stand it.

The Little Disturbances
of the White Middle Class

I 'm no therapist, believe me. I think you have to be crazy to be one. That is, I think you wouldn't become one if you weren't always trying to fix something broken in yourself.

One of my more mixed-up students is an art therapist in a mental hospital. This morning she drew a picture of me for her patients and they all calmed down. Didn't make me feel any better.

No sooner had she phoned me with this tidbit when the phone rang again. It was a friend in the West who was having trouble with his wife and was so upset that he could form only half a sentence before he lost heart. I finished his sentences for him. He at last said he felt better. I fixed myself a drink.

There was the phone again. Another student of mine said he was so depressed about being rejected from seven graduate poetry programs that he was thinking of killing himself. "They are doing you a favor," I told him. "No poet ever came out of poetry schools." That made *him* happy but it totally freaked me: I teach in one. I topped off the ice in my whiskey glass with some more whiskey and ripped the phone from the wall.

I hadn't yet read the day's mail so I sank into my easy chair with the stack. I opened a letter from my friend H. in New York, a very witty woman who's always on top of it. She once even wrote a self-help book for the sexually timid. "I don't know if it's just the squalor of New York," began her letter, "or the fact that everybody's getting old, but I'm not feeling very well lately." I plugged my phone back in and called her. She was in, on a Saturday night. "I just had a date with a millionaire," she said. "We watched the Mets game on his huge TV, then he sent me home with his chauffeur at ten o'clock." "Call the chauffeur," I advised her. That cheered her up. She said she would.

Listen to us, I thought. Poor middle-class misfits. We turn to each other, each of us equally neurotic, and talk, or write, as if that might help. Funny thing is, it seems to. I see that Abby's column in Chicago is up for grabs, should the right optimistic-yet-wary person qualify. I would apply if I thought I was sufficiently wary. I am, however, profoundly optimistic. I believe, like the Buddhists, that life is sorrow. We can only go up from here.

Today We List, Tomorrow We Fall

T omorrow, go without a list. Then try it for another day. See if you can go three days without a list. A week. A month. A year. If you can go a year without a list, congratulations! You will notice improvements in your memory. You will remember the things you have to make lists of today, including maybe what it is you're doing on this planet.

One day humanity will kick the list-making habit. That day, says my friend Bandido the anti-listmaker, we'll be back on track. Bandido, who changes names every time he has a new show, has dedicated his art to the eradication of lists. The way he sees it, man is the list-making animal. We list everything: who we know, what we have, what we hope to do. Community and religion are made fast by lists, from records of births and deaths to laws regulating conduct. Paleolithic hunter-gatherers no doubt listed their ancestors and progeniture, and maybe the kinds of animals they ate. But it wasn't until the Neolithic, with agriculture and property, that list making really took off. Property may in fact have never existed without list making: noting it brought it into existence. Marking down what one had became proof that one had it. At first it must have been simply a desire to record communal and individual holdings in order to know exactly what was missing after a raid or a storm. Later, it became a way for the community to keep track of what an individual had so it could tax the holdings. Government is the product of lists, history the scrutiny of them.

Bandido concedes that some lists are good poetry. Thoreau's lists of expenditures in *Walden* are prescriptions for the simple life. Of course, they're nostalgic lists: two extra jobs would be needed to pay for the same simple things these days. The ironic poetry of the supermarket shopping list is also exemplary anthropology: the diet of *Homo Americanus*.

We are list-making animals, repeats Bandido, but the extent to which we have taken this disposition is extreme. We are about to be swallowed by our lists, he says, by their incredible size, their immense power. The more of us there are, the more we do, the more we have, the more we list. What was once simple desire to remember has now become mandatory, a time-consuming activity that absorbs us. We are not even making lists of real things anymore: we are making lists of lists. With computers we can now surpass our best abilities. And when everything at last is listed, humans will go out of business because making a list will be all they know how to do. Give it up, warns Bandido. Either we forget everything now and get rid of all the lists or we'll become wandering shades in a hell of speeding ciphers.

I thanked Bandido and made a list of his warnings to use in this essay.

Virus from Space

T wo Australian scientists have found that on its last swing past our planet, Halley's comet sprayed it with organic material. They have used their findings to support their theory that germs and viruses come from outer space. At almost the same time, the Department of Agriculture, which is located on Earth, granted a Nebraska company the world's first license to market a living, genetically altered virus. If all viruses came from outer space until now, they will no longer do so, unless all our genetic engineers decide to relocate in outer space and mail in their viruses from there.

I have no idea what the Australians base their outer space theory on, but they are right in line with ancient thinking on the matter. The Egyptians pointed their pyramids at the stars, which they believed to be the source of all life, just as did the Mayas and the Aztecs. The scriveners of myth from Gilgamesh to the newest science fiction novels invariably point their teleological compasses at the stars. Some storytellers fear the life-spewing sky and are convinced that the invaders are hostile. Others have a feeling of awe about it and encourage worship.

These imaginative pictures of the sky clash fundamentally with the other, scientific picture that space exploration, manned and unmanned, has been showing us, which is that of a universe composed of inert gases, dead rocks, and ice. The only life in outer space, according to our instruments, is us. Ours are the only germs and viruses hurtling forth through the chill of the near cosmos. No astronaut has so far come back organically different.

Who's right?

Is Halley's comet a genetically altered organism released by the Agriculture Department to two Australian scientists?

Or is the U.S. Agriculture Department itself a genetically altered organism released from outer space with special powers to spread germs and viruses?

Where *is* outer space, anyway?

Punk Nostalgia

R iding home from the movies, I had a conversation on the bus with a clean-cut young stranger. "They don't make music like they used to," he said.

"Pardon me?"

"Music. You know. Like punk."

"Yeah," I said. "And they sure don't make people like Sid and Nancy anymore either." We had both just viewed the rise and fall of last week's favorite heroic couple, the two punk junkies whose vocabularies consisted of fifteen words max.

"I used to have a Mohawk," my benchmate confessed.

"What happened?" I said.

"Gave it up for art administration," he replied. "I'm an art administrator for one of our larger art organizations."

Poor Sid! Poor Nancy! Dead in New York of youthful rebellion and dirty needles, being missed by art administrators! That's double death, if you ask me.

"Did you ever see the Sex Pistols?" I asked.

"Gawd!" he cried. "I would have loved to!"

I rose slightly above him in omnipotent cultural superiority. "*I* did! Saw 'em in San Francisco and was right up front until I figured I'd better skiddoo before I was totally drenched in spit and cut by flying beer bottles!"

"That must have been *something*!" cried the art administrator.

"It was," I said. "I had to take several showers afterward, and I still wake up screaming! I have flashbacks!"

"*Flashbacks!*" He could barely hold his admiration in check. I could see that he was traversed by nostalgia for his bygone blitzed-out days of punk amnesia.

"That's the trouble with memory," I said. "If you don't wipe it out totally right when you do something memorable, it's bound to come back as flashbacks."

"Like history," he said. "The first time around it's serious, the second time it's parody."

"No," I insisted. "The second time around it's a *flashback*."

We fell silent for a while as the bus pulled into Metairie to unload hospital supplies from Baton Rouge. My companion seemed to be meditating on a past when his Mohawk cut clean through the fog of history. I pondered the budget of his organization and wondered how much he'd shell out for a performance by me next month, when I will be broke. Maybe something called "Punk Flashbacks," a long set with poetry, peach brandy, and spit.

"Peace Through Vandalism"

I saw this graffito sprayed on the halls of the building where I teach: PEACE THROUGH VANDALISM. Things are a bit slow to reach us here in the very deep delta and graffiti has been one of them. The subways and walls of New York have been graffitoed for decades and the best vandals have long since sold out to the galleries uptown. Here, however, the medium is novel. And the message would be intriguing anywhere: PEACE THROUGH VANDALISM. I had been looking down this boring hallway for several years and was beginning to feel something akin to comfort, if not peace, in its seeming unchangeability. It was utterly familiar to me. It even gave me a sense of slightly swelling self-importance as I, the powerful professor, strode down it amidst parting masses of peasants, I mean students. I had been well on my way to inner peace through swelling of the ego before seeing this sign. But these very same walls and their predictable monotony must have signified pain and anxiety to the masses I parted on my way to Parnassus, I mean my office. But now, post-sign, I began to shrink considerably. The "vandalism" in question made me anxious while it comforted the masses. The "peace" it meant to invoke was "peace" for the oppressed. To the powers-that-be it was anxious disruption—downright strife, in fact. If the vandals were allowed to continue in this way they would tear apart "the fabric of society," making just enough holes in it for the barrels of guns to stick through. Remember, peasants, it is only this endlessly washable, eminently stretchable fabric that stands between your peace and ours.

In my youth, I too had been a vandal. I once spray-painted the back of the replica of Rodin's *The Thinker* in front of the Detroit Art Museum with these provocative words: WHAT'S THIS PIG THINKING ABOUT? THE TIME FOR REVOLUTION IS NOW!

I remember that a few years earlier the cube sculpture at Cooper Square in New York had these sprayed words on it: GIVE ME LITHIUM OR GIVE ME METH. I was young then, so I knew what they meant. And now that I think of it, it is not the students' graphic vandalism that filled me with dread, but their youth. My own, now vandalized by the self-important professor, poked its head out at the sign. Next day, of course, the sign was gone. Janitorial staff had been wakened in the middle of the night and made to erase furiously all traces of youth.

But remember, profs, writing itself began as graffiti. The species, in fact, began its rapid ascent to *Homo Scriber* by daubing pictures on the walls of caves. Our pictures got smaller, until they became symbols; words are only the miniaturized abstractions of cave wall pictures. Some cultures, like Chinese, still use pictures to stand in for things. But we, we have forgotten our beginnings. The cave walls have been replaced by the book, and pictures on walls we now call art. In so doing we have lost something, namely, the use of our dwellings to communicate our insights. Along with graffiti, the refrigerator note is one of the few remaining traces of that once noble tradition. "Gone shopping, dear. May never return. The cat's been murdered. I unplugged the clock."'

Books, sorry to say, have made most messages boring. In opening a book one is reasonably sure that nothing in it will jump out to cover the wall. If there is something shocking in the book, one can quickly close it. It's easier even than turning off the TV. But the future is, I'm afraid, in graffiti rather than books. Books have been growing ever more loosely bound, going from hardbacks to paperbacks and now to software. They have also gotten more expensive in the process. The day is coming, however, when books will become completely unbound in graffiti and, at last, be free. Already, our citizenry does more reading on billboards and T-shirts than it does in books. Very soon it will be reading only freshly sprayed walls. The anxiety of culture will disappear. PEACE THROUGH VANDALISM will overcome one and all.

Get your spray can now.

The Healthy Crank

I have always considered myself a generous fellow. I was therefore surprised to hear someone tell me, "You're always complaining about one thing or another." Am I? And if so, are things so hunky-dory that one ought to acknowledge only their golden beams? Speaking, I argue, is in itself an act of criticism, an acknowledgment that things are not perfect, that problems need to be communicated. Perfection does not need communication: the temperature is always right in the womb. A person's first speech, which is a baby's cry, calls attention to the fact that conditions are no longer ideal. From one's first bellowing breath, one opens one's mouth to fix the world: to explain one's side, to point out imbalances, to protest. Angels are silent because they are happy. Humans speak because they are not. And I have proof now, if any were needed, that we are perfectly right to do so.

A psychologist at Southern Methodist University says that airing out personal traumas is good for the body's immune system. In his study, fifty students who regularly wrote about their own painful experiences showed increased lymphocyte response and went to the doctor a lot less often than did fifty others who wrote only on assigned topics. Clearly, complaining is good for you. So is being personally involved in what's wrong in the world. And this is also clearly why the so-called Silent Majority is sick. Instead of personal traumas, most people are content with TV traumas. Instead of expressing personal opinions on what's wrong in their own words, they allow themselves to be surveyed to death. Our collective immune system has been weakened by television and the public opinion poll. So many people speak for us, we are giving up the hope of participating in the general conversation. That can't be good for our immune system, which is not only a defense against things that are bad for us but also a marker of our own individual boundaries. It points out where we end and the world begins. If others speak for us, we cannot tell what is rightly ours. Which is exactly how they rob us.

I'm speaking for you right now, am I not?

Inside the Commentary

H ere is a glimpse inside a commentator's head, for those of you who want to follow in my footsteps.

8:00 A.M. I wake to a perfectly empty, though slightly aching head. Scan backward for dreams and find that I have dreamed of millions of fast-moving toys climbing rapidly to the tops of mountains. The dream resembles a battery commercial. Is there an idea in it? For Madison Avenue, maybe, but not for me.

9:30. Having read eight newspapers in seven languages and carefully cut out stories, I spread these before me and contemplate. New TV-beam toys are being unveiled at a toy fair. These toys respond to high-frequency signals emanating from a television set: they spin, scream, and fly when the TV tells them to. Consumer groups oppose such toys because they will create a new class of kids even more attached to their sets than they already are. I scan my moral spectrum: Am I for or against these devices? You would expect me to be against them, which inclines me to be for them. After all, I already believe that we are manipulated by TV signals that tell us everything we don't need to know so that we can keep on quietly consuming. On the other hand, kids are always whom these signals try to break down, so I have to stand up for them. But the whole thing bores me before my coffee is cold. Discard.

9:45. Another story tells about some Christians burying the Devil in an elaborate ceremony in their local church. It's a lovely story, full of potential trills for my native wit, but it's essentially soulless: its only point is that people are dimwits, though not devoid of charm.

10:00. I throw out the newspapers and go back to humans. Last night a friend of mine told me that self-portraits are the only kind of painting still interesting to her. "Let's face it," she said, "the mirror is the best art." "Sure," I said, "if you find yourself fascinating." I rarely do, and then only when I'm being interviewed. Then I get to make myself up into the fascinating person I never knew I was.

11:00. I turn on the radio to a country-and-western station. Human emotion pours out. C & W has that covered. Only one source left: the streets of my lovely town. Might as well go out, see what's shaking in that vast universe neither song nor paper has found yet.

My story waits for me in a little café.

The Weight of the World

I try to stay light. But the world is heavy. When I was young I woke up at a certain comfortable hour, let's say noon, and unrolled my *San Francisco Chronicle*. On the front page there used to be wonderful news: THE UNIVERSE FLOWS BACKWARDS, ASTRONOMERS SAY. It made me grin over my one piece of dry toast with poached egg. As long as the universe flowed backwards and I got up at noon, there seemed to be no weight in the world. Nor was there any weight on me, as my poached egg could testify. Youth was light and old age heavy. Pleasure had wings. Everything else was a drag. The spirit played lightly over the pages of the paper and almost every word turned into poetry.

Things are different now. I woke up at six this morning and found in my *Times-Picayune* that the world is full of dark matter and it is going to collapse from its immense gravity. I can barely get down my fried eggs and grits for the weight of this news. Previously seen arcs of light that span cosmic oceans turn out to be "optical illusions" indicating not light but heaviness. Everywhere, in the endless ether, there are squatting brown dwarfs, black holes, collapsed eons of matter.

And then the phone began to ring. On the other end were not my sweet, light friends who once needed my help to figure out how to fill the delicious emptiness of time, but professional associates who want me to fulfill obligations for which oceans of time are barely sufficient. The once-empty egg of time is now jammed full of the weight of duty. I am reminded of the gentle but firm way in which the poet Robert Creeley likes to introduce unpleasant but necessary propositions: "Not heavily, but. . . . " In other words, "I don't really want to place the burden of this misery on your winged shoulders, but there it is, buddy, the world. . . . "

Silence and solitude, once the guarantors of lightness, have made way for words and encounters, the demons of weight. Milan Kundera, in a wonderful book called *The Unbearable Lightness of Being*, posits the problems of our world between the opposing poles of lightness and weight. Art is light and politics is heavy, he says, and the irony of it all is that lightness turns into weight but never does weight become lightness unless one goes mad. Madness is a kind of lightness but it's a rather heavy solution. Kundera's artists begin lightly but soon enough the heavy hand of the State is upon them. Children likewise begin in sweet weightlessness, and then we bury them in books and chop them to pieces with the hands of the clock. It would be best perhaps to remain children or poets, but then comes the phone and the newspaper and the rent.

For the longest time, I refused to carry anything heavier than a pencil and a thin notebook. And wherever I went I saw people likewise swinging lightly on the balls of their feet with only the merest accoutrements. I now lug a briefcase, books, papers, several pens, and, God help me, a portable computer. Poetry, I used to say, is the loveliest of arts because all you need for it is your wrist, a razor blade and a wall. But these days even poetry goes about carrying the baggage of time. And my body, like the cosmos, contains more dark matter than I originally thought. Inside everyone there turns a radar, ever so softly. It knows what we have forgotten: that we were made to fly. That in the body there turns yet the propeller of light. I now and then take a reading from it when things stay still long enough. Meanwhile, I stay away from scales. The news is not good.

"What's the Frequency, Kenneth?"

It's ancient history as far as the news goes, but it's still on my mind, the attack on Dan Rather by two New York City men who, while they punched him out, kept repeating, "What's the frequency, Kenneth?" Rather told his assailants that they had the wrong man, but the suspicion gnaws at me that "Kenneth" just may be the name of that demon that hides inside all of us media people. All the news you hear comes from Kenneth. Kenneth is plugged in to the central frequency of the world brain, whence he gets the stuff he spews on the world. A newsman is only a gate, a door through which Kenneth's news is funneled to the public. In this respect, it is not coincidental that a doorman saved Rather from further battering: his job is to look after doors. Kenneth, on the other hand, is more like a building manager: he decides what should and shouldn't go through the door.

Most of us media types are unaware that Kenneth lives inside us and gives all the orders. The general public, bewildered by all the bad news, would love to get their hands on Kenneth. They'd do anything to find his frequency. The two men who assailed the newsman are the John Q. Public of the 1980s. They are very different from the Chicago cops who beat up Rather in 1968. That beating was comprehensible and it showed Rather to be a man of courage, the line on his resumé that landed him his current job. The 1986 meeting cannot be understood in the simple political terms of 1968. In 1968 it was possible to blame the newsman for the news, attack the door as if it were the whole building. These days, it's what's behind the door that upsets everyone. Kenneth is there.

I'm afraid that the New York attack is not an isolated incident. The graffiti is still there in the subway: WHAT'S THE FREQUENCY, KENNETH? And the two dudes who used to ride my line and used to slap each other five and say, "WHAT'S THE HAPS, BABY?" have changed their greeting to "WHAT'S THE FREQUENCY, KENNETH?"

I hope it doesn't get out of hand.

Follow-ups

"What happened afterwards?" So asks my child after I contrive an end to my bedtime story. He wants to know what happened after all that happened happened. "There are so many stories in this world," I tell him, "that some of them just have to end. Some of them, it's true, just won't go away—they'll turn up over and over in sequels and further episodes. But this isn't one of them, Son. Good night." When he does sleep, it occurs to me that he is not the only one unhappy that stories come and go with nary a word of what happens next.

There are few follow-ups to the stories we read or hear. What happened to the man who forged the Hitler diaries? Or the man who faked the autobiography of the pope? Did the pope forgive him when he came to America, the way he forgave his would-be assassin? Or is faking a life story worse than attempting to end it? These are stories that interest me because I am a writer. But perhaps *all* the dread and foreboding most of us feel is brought about by the lack of follow-up. Not knowing how most stories ended—or *will* end—leaves most of us in an anxious state.

Not long ago we had this Harmonic Convergence, which may have been less an attempt at cosmic harmony than an attempt to end the old story and begin a new one. One cycle is ending and another beginning: How many times have we heard this tale, from the micro- to the macrocosm? But how to know precisely where the scale applies and what the laws are? Was the Convergence successful? There was no follow-up in the media. But in my heart I feel that something indeed happened, that a nameless new story is about to unfold. As I look about me, the tone of the times is ominous. The texture of the news is rough, made from the substance of war, religion, famine, environmental disaster.

My son turns in his sleep. He is dreaming about what happens next. And so do we all. When there are no factual follow-ups to stories, we finish them in our dreams. The stories continue to lead a life in our psyches, to be reborn as new and incredible facts.

Isn't the Pope himself a follow-up to the medieval story, oddly placed within this new era of capitalism? Watching him on TV in full regalia, surrounded by masses of worshipers, I had the uncomfortable feeling that time had stood still for ten centuries. Here was the absolute ruler demanding total obedience, silence, and adoration. We could have been anywhere in the long history of the world, joined in an immense and wordless despair. The only difference was that I was watching everything on TV, a measure more of slight distance than of actual progress. I was welded through my eyes to the throng.

The same pictures greet us daily, though they are of varying degrees of goodness and legitimacy. Religious leaders, fanatics, zealots lead quiescent masses away from reason and democracy; the eighteenth, nineteenth, and twentieth centuries seem to be receding before ages past when the unsettled masses looked for salvation from another source. History in crisis brings with it the wish for supernatural help. In the year 1000, followers of prophets, rabbis, seers, alchemists, and forgotten cranks brought the world to a standstill. Eyes upturned, they waited for the lightning that would signal the end of matter. We are now on the momentous threshold again, only the lightning that would end all matter is within our grasp. We are approaching the end of our millennium with our hearts full of unfinished stories. The apocalypse promised by all the millennial fanatics of our time, from the Harmonic Convergers to the Ayatollah, is the wish for an end to these unresolved stories.

I pray that the prophets are wrong and that ours is an endless story. And that the millennium is just a convention like a paragraph space in a book. And that when my son wakes, the old story will continue.

The Lord's Corporations

There are psychic disturbances loose in the world, big winds that blow through the collective unconsciousness, gathering strength. Our humble souls are wracked by them. What is one to make of the TV ministries of the Lord looking to swallow one another like deregulated airlines? Are the Lord's airplanes stalled on the airports of the media? Are the religious wars raging elsewhere out there about to break out at home in front of the children? Preachers retire to towers to fast until death unless they can collect millions from us. But what if death isn't enough, and upon dying they find the next world equally unforthcoming? Dying used to be a sure way to meet your maker. But now, with so many dying for religious reasons in Iran and elsewhere, the hereafter might be one big traffic jam with believers of all sorts fighting to get to different levels. There may even be, God forbid, a whole class of agnostic spirits who fancy themselves scientific and won't believe in anything even when dead. What avail death to a dead televangelist if he finds that the postmodern spilleth into the postmortem? Pity, pity the troubled man of today's electronic cloth.

Some say that televangelism is the Devil playing fast and loose with the wealth of the faithful. Others say that it's only capitalism reaching at last the heavenly realms on ladders of cash, the way McDonald's reached infinity on mountains of burgers. Still others say that the new corporations of the Lord were made *ex nihilo*; that, like the world, they came out of nothing and are about to return there. But we, the faithful and the humble, who have neither towers nor TV satellites to turn to, feel only the blowing of the winds of insecurity and fear. The day of reckoning may be at hand: first the preachers are borne on the wings of evil, then their TV soap operas stop showing up. Truly will darkness then descend upon the world.

A Modest Proposal

The following is an open letter to the Reverend Messrs. Bakker, Falwell, and Swaggart.

Dear Jim, Jerry, and Jimmy,

I think I know a way to help you redeem the current crisis of TV evangelism that threatens to engulf your media empires. What I am proposing is that you use your enormous influence to enlarge the sphere of your moral concerns. I realize how vulnerable you have become in the one area that has been your bread and butter for several years now, that of issues concerning private morality and the integrity of the family. I do not suggest abandoning your crusade to make us better moral human beings put here by God to do the right thing, but I urge you to take your inspiration a little further to include the welfare of the whole species. In short, I urge you to combine environmental concerns with private ones. What use is your fight for the rights of unborn babies if children die of cancers brought about by industrial pollution?

How may times have you gotten up on a glorious, God-given morning in Baton Rouge, Reverend Swaggart, only to be nauseated by the chemical smell of refineries and fertilizer plants? Your power is great in the South but think how much greater it would be if you joined forces with that other great but equally limited regional power, namely, the Garden Club? All those folks who gather together for the purpose of making their backyards perfect could be moved to make the whole earth into God's garden.

And you, Reverend Bakker, whose sexual history seems to me nothing if not a desire to return to the Garden of Eden, couldn't you lead us all back to the Garden? The Devil is alive and well, as you have told us many times, but isn't his real name vinyl chloride and benzene? We may yet be saved if you but rename the end of the world. And folks will continue to reach for their purses, if they can find them in the smog.

And you, Reverend Falwell, upon whose shoulders rests the burden of several million white-middle-class souls, each one with a private backyard and a BBQ pit, wouldn't you be moving your faithful closer to salvation by keeping chemical fertilizer off those lawns and hormones out of the beef about to be BBQed? A lower cancer rate among your parishioners would ensure that they be fruitful and multiply to the greater glory and longevity of your church.

Seize the hour, you righteous angels of the Lord, and join up against the polluters of beaches and the true murderers of children. You have nothing to lose but your right wings. Since you never fly anyway, what use have you of them? Your mission's here on earth, as long as there is one.

The Rock Garden

My student wrote a poem divided exactly in half, like a demonstration grapefruit. The first half talked about a past life of sin. The girl who "just wants to have fun," that was me, that half said. The other half said that now she was in the light of heaven, and that the main question people will be asked when the day comes is, "Do you know the Son of God?" The first and sinful half was full of particular details. The second was vague and steamy like the tear-laden air of a gospel tent. I wouldn't have wanted to be in her shoes these past few months that saw the fall of Jim Bakker, Marvin Gorman, and now her guru, Jimmy Swaggart. (Of course I couldn't have gotten *into* her shoes, but that's another story.)

The betrayal of the faith by its living incarnation is a devastating blow to a believer. Divine spokesmen are allowed to be human only up to a point: they can turn each other in like any other corporate sharks, they can sling stones in the garden, they can display awesome bad taste and wealth, they can wring their followers' wallets bone-dry, they can even dress up their wives like tarts in a Fellini outtake—but they cannot, *they cannot* have sex with strangers. This is the deal even for secular leaders now. Nobody could watch Gary Hart shaking hands and kissing babies on TV without wondering where those hands and lips had been. It's even worse for preachers, who have to lay hands upon many afflicted parts.

I do feel sorry for my student, though. She will lose some faith and that always hurts, and she might even lose her job if she is one of the thousands of people Swaggart's religious empire employs. The times are bad and evangelism has been a thriving business. I hear Jim Bakker's parents just applied for unemployment. That's the problem with the Judeo-Christian God, ultimately: it's a one-boss system. When the boss goes, the whole tribe is lost. The Greeks were smart, I told my student: they had more gods than there were things for, and whenever there was something new in the world they put a god in it to keep it sane. "Sure," she said, "but they were pagans." "Maybe so," I said, "but they still had gods. You want that I should call Nietzsche?"

A few years ago I would have had no trouble calling Nietzsche. ("Herr Professor Nietzsche? Can you tell this student please that God is dead?" *"Gott is Todt."* "Thank you, Herr Professor Nietzsche.") But that was a long time ago. Since Nietzsche declared the death of God, God's come back several times, no time stronger than in the last decade. Christian, Jewish, and Islamic fundamentalism have risen on a scale inconceivable to the rather radical founders of modern republics. Most college professors find themselves in the unenviable position of spoilers at a party. The students are having a merry old time floating and bobbing on the current of the deity. The old enlightenment props of reason and doubt are but flotsam and debris.

The marriage of radio and religion gave rise to the Ayatollah Khomeini. The TV evangelists of America are also coming close to seizing political power. Is this the age of false prophets so aptly described in Revelations? But then Dostoevsky thought that it was his age, the nineteenth century, that John meant. And before that, Sabbatai Zevi and his followers thought the end was coming in the year 1000. Whatever the frame, there is no doubt that we are living in an age of millennial hysteria. Fortunately, millennialism has its own corrective built into it: sin. Evangelists, too, "just want to have fun," and their fall is a healthy antidote to mass delirium. The madness of crowds was never a pretty sight, and I would rather the new false Messiahs trip on their own shoelaces than be accidentally or intentionally martyred.

The Opening of the
American Sentence

T here is a book on the best-seller list called *The Closing of the American Mind* that argues that we should all go back to learning Greek and Latin before our minds close. I'm afraid we might just lose our minds entirely if we filled them with dead languages. The best-seller list isn't the only thing that warns of the dire consequences of today's undergraduate curriculum. A memo at my school warns against the sins most often committed by students against the English language. Watch out for the "gross reference": "Bill hit Fred on the head with the bat. It was hard. It made him mad." Well, I don't know how "gross" this is. If I were Fred I'd be mad too, and I'd jump a few logical steps to get back at that hooligan Bill. Then there is, of course, the ever-threatening "dangling modifier": "While thinking about Sue, the Honda hit the fence." "John ran to the door and yelled at the dog in his underwear." Being somewhat familiar with how students live nowadays, I can see the dog wearing John's underwear. In fact, I saw it late last night. The memo also warns of the "double negative": "I can't hardly believe it." "I can't get no satisfaction." Come now. Are the Rolling Stones wrong? Everybody knows that they opened the American mind wider than any Greeks whose names I can't just now recall.

I can't help thinking, amid all the neo-ancient plaints, that my students' minds are open far wider than the best-seller list imagines. I mean, nobody stays up till 4:00 A.M. putting under-wear on a dog without some complex, though no doubt nonlin-ear, thought at work. Such things are done the way my students do everything else: to a soundtrack. Their every move is made to the sound of some line like, "My name is MCA, I have a license to kill," from the Beastie Boys, which is an interesting update of "Freedom's just another word for nothing left to lose," which ran through my head when I was their age. The difference, if there is any, is that the American mind has since had to make room for Colonel Sanders and Colonel North and MTV. With so much in their heads, the emptying of the mind might be in order. Given that necessity, it's a wonder they'll still resort to just the double negative. A triple negative isn't even enough if you don't get no further than *that*.

Sacred Cows

What's happening to the sacred cow? A black-and-white one with the word *REAGAN* painted red on its side was recently torn to pieces by a frenzied crowd in Tripoli under the eyes of Muammar Khaddafi. A student of ancient religions may note with wonder this event, which marks the resurrection of the cult of Mithra in the Middle East.

Mithra was the secret religion of the Roman legions for over a thousand years. It was a sun-worshiping cult practiced underground, and its chief mystery was the slaughter of the bull. The return of Mithra is not incidental. The old gods return when great disturbances rupture the crust of our more modernly entrenched beliefs. The raging bull tearing through the fabric of the twentieth century is being whipped by the demon of an even older practice, the Jihad, or Holy War. The Jihad is war without rules. For many centuries now we have created a delicate web of rules about war, aimed at acknowledging principles higher than sheer murder. But the dimensions of Holy War in the atomic age are obviously inconceivable, and the sacrifice of the bull is a disquieting symbol.

A reasonable person may also note that in this, our year of the Lord 1986, the Agriculture Department of the United States has announced that dairy farmers will send nearly a million cows to the slaughterhouse over the next eighteen months in an effort to curb the nation's milk surplus. These nonsymbolic cows, going to their anonymous slaughter, are fundamentally different from the highly visible bull of Tripoli. But the quiet cows are no less symbolic of our century in their orderly departure for the heavenly pastures. Our century is characterized by both the high visibility of symbols and the quiet, bureaucratic, *en masse* dispatchment of beings from earth. Protected by the glaring light

of symbolic exhibitions, the gray men, the good little bureau-
crats, work undisturbed at their mechanical jobs. Seeing how
much mileage Khaddafi can get out of a single cow, think how
much we can get out of a million. I think we should use each
and every one of these quietly doomed cows symbolically: we
should paint the name of a doomsday weapon on the side of
each one just before slaughter, and make a media event out of it.
Colonel Khaddafi has something there.

Used Dictators

Almost nobody wants a used dictator. Look at poor Baby Doc: shunned like a bag of bad gris-gris. He owns houses in France but France won't let him live in them. He wants to emigrate to the United States but our dictator quota for the year has been filled. Of course, it's all a game to fool those who'd have his hide. The truth is that Baby Doc knows well where he's headed for. It's a tiny mountainous region in the no-man's-land between the borders of two powerful nations. It's a pretty place, filled with innocent-looking bungalows. It has no official name, though some call it Tyrannia—not to be confused with Tyranna, the capital of Albania, though it resembles Albania in that so little news comes out of it. All we know is this: in Tyrannia a great many experiments are being conducted by countries too ashamed to be openly associated with formerly absolute rulers.

One of these experiments concerns the removal of certain substances from the brains of used dictators to see if a serum could be manufactured to inoculate people against an excessive appetite for power. That's noble. Another experiment has the ex-dictators developing the artistic talents that they all, without exception, had before the world rejected them and they were forced to become dictators. Hitler's meager watercolor palette, Napoleon's sentimental poetry, and Franco's warped pottery are being improved and transcended here, as well as performed and displayed day and night in the quaint little plaza with its flower-bedecked machine-gun turrets.

Baby Doc's bungalow has been ready for his arrival since the day he took power. One of the niftier features of Tyrannia is that it expects all dictators eventually, no matter how powerful they seem. Another is that Tyrannia is nonideological. Castro has a bungalow waiting for him here, right next door to Franco's.

That's yet another neat feature: there is no recognition of death in Tyrannia. Stalin, Attila the Hun, Díaz, and Mussolini all live in harmonious cement bunkers filled with electronics. They play canasta or watch videotapes of mass murders and tortures. Some prefer one, some the other.

Excitement is high in Tyrannia today: both Baby Doc and Ferdinand Marcos are expected to arrive sometime around noon. Whose pillows would you like to see plumped up next?

Military Jealousy

Are our military men jealous of their South American counterparts? After all, the military men of Bolivia, Ecuador, and Paraguay are proudly strutting about in their finery while holding their countries in their iron fists. Is it possible that because of our proximity to South America we may gravitate more easily toward its style than toward parliamentary Europe which is, after all, very far away? There are some who maintain that not long after Eisenhower warned us about the dangers of the "military-industrial complex," the complex *did* take over. It did so quietly at just about the time of the Kennedy assassination, and we've been in its good keeping ever since. So as not to unduly alarm the populace, civilians still "lead" the country. Now and then, an imperial president like Richard Nixon will attempt to dress the palace guard in regal Latin style, but the public outcry puts a quick end to that. But when Nixon himself was finished, it was time for General Haig to step in and take command. When President Reagan was wounded, the General told the rest of us, "I'm in charge!" It was never clear to me whether he meant that he was in charge of the situation then developing, or that he had been in charge all along, so not to worry.

Now that Colonel North has emerged from the shadows, it does appear that a new generation of military man is becoming restless, South American style. Colonels will be colonels. They want the whole world to see them in their uniforms. Why should they hide behind men in suits? Why should our good-looking colonels not strut their stuff like the Paraguayan brass? It is true that Brazil and Argentina are now run by men in suits, but for how long? Civilians, even when acting for the military, are bound to get bogged down in legalities. At this point it might be difficult for General Haig and Colonel North to run for office on the same ticket.

On the other hand, who needs to run?

Step Down, America

Senator Joseph Biden set a wonderful precedent by dropping out of the 1988 presidential race for mouthing other people's words. I wish that all of us, following his inspired example, would resign from whatever we are involved in. The words the senator was accused of stealing had not belonged to the people he stole them from in any case. They were the words of ghostwriters bought and paid for. The ghostwriters themselves didn't have to dig deeper than their store of clichés. And clichés, as everyone knows, are free for the taking. They're what most people use instead of thought.

But things are now changed. Senator Biden's example bids us all to resign from getting where we've gotten by mouthing clichés. First, all the other politicians will have to go. Most of them speak two equally unoriginal languages: a deceitful one to fool us and a filthy one to amuse their buddies. (In this respect, Nixon was perhaps our greatest bilingual politician.) Then it's the professionals' turn. Lawyers cite precedents and make speeches that sound exactly like other speeches. Engineers endeavor to repeat exactly the formulas and techniques others have used. Novelists write the same novel over and over again. Teachers repeat the same lesson. Students write the same paper. The newspaper runs the same news day after day. Art has always copied something, first nature, then itself. Postmodern art and literature revel in unattributed quotation. Political leaders are mostly copies of one another. The last remaining differences among them reside in something in the DNA that science is trying to eliminate through cloning. We eat fake vegetables and drink simulated juices. We dress alike. People imitate pictures in magazines that imitate pictures in other magazines.

You want something original? It's being faked as we speak. Faking originals is the biggest business now going. Our postmodern age is the age of the copy *par excellence*. Senator Biden has shown us it's possible to resign from it. He is our first post-postmodern public man.

The Passive Voice

A colleague at LSU, Don Moore, points out that the passive voice is getting a big workout these days. He cites President Reagan, who said, "The execution was flawed and mistakes were made." All by itself, it seems, the execution was flawed. And about these mistakes—Who made them? We will never know. That is the beauty of the passive voice. It exists for the purpose of describing phenomena in a vacuum, phenomena that have nothing to do with the speaker. The speaker merely reports the facts in the way a bagman's lawyer describes a liquor store fire: "The floor was littered with oily rags, but arson is not suspected."

Who does the passive voice belong to if the speaker does not wish to be associated with the content of what is said? Does it somehow come from somewhere *outside* the speaker? In Mr. Reagan's case, did it come from behind him, below him, or through him? Did it come from Colonel North, who uses so many voices? The military is a well-known user of the passive voice. "A five-thousand-dollar screw was wrongly charged to the army." "A bloodless coup has taken place." The passive voice is the ventriloquist's voice. Is the president a dummy? A hologram? If the voice doesn't come from the military, where does it come from? Outer space? God? Maybe the passive voice is on tape in an emergency vault; whenever there is a crisis, the president lip-synchs.

When the passive voice isn't speaking, absurdity is. Take the contras, for instance. *Contra* means "anti." The other day we had anti-contra demonstrators, or anti-antis. And on the same day there were counter-anti-contra demonstrators, or anti-anti-antis. Doesn't anybody say "I am for" anymore?

Big Joke

R onald Reagan's war on drugs is the biggest joke since Gerry Ford's WIN button. Ford wanted us to whip inflation by wearing a button. Reagan wants us to quit using chemicals by making war on pills and powders. Alas! Everybody in America is a substance abuser. More than half of all Americans are overweight, clearly macaroni abusers. Some of these macaroni abusers try to get off their carbohydrate habit with pills. Half of these overweight Americans are killed by the other half who are on booze and drunk and just waiting to spread abuse around. A friend of mine says that as America goes quickly to the Right, the only stabilizing forces in the political arena are McDonald's and Coca-Cola, who emerge oddly neutral because they feed everybody, no matter what their politics. Of course. But has anyone looked into the substance abuse problem as concerns the cow, Holy Source of Hamburgers? Abusers of hormones and chemicals, these cows stream into the obese, drunk bodies of Right-leaning Americans, bearing more drugs than flow across the Mexican border. And at last the old rumor is verified: the taste of Coca-Cola does indeed depend upon the essence of leaves from the coca plant. If it's a war on drugs we're waging here, then every drug is the enemy. So let's stop Coca-Cola and McDonald's from funneling these drugs into the New-Right-War-on-Drugs Body Politic of the New America.

The sorry fact is you can't even get through traffic these days without being a horrid abuser. You abuse gasoline and then abuse the body of earth by belching exhaust right into its face. You abuse yourself when you don't have anyone else to abuse, and you find your way through the maze of daily life by abusing the substance of every living and nonliving thing in your path. Tell me where you live and I'll tell you what and how much you abuse. Say, for instance, that you live in the White House and have just declared a war on drugs. Well, you've just abused a few million gullible folks, killed thousands of trees on account of the ink spilled on the subject, and abused my giggle center in the bargain. And I'll stop right there: I won't abuse the muse.

I bought a book on pills at my local bookstore to see what the enemy looks like, or at least that division of the enemy that comes in pill form. *The Pill Book: The Illustrated Guide to the Most Prescribed Drugs in the United States* has pictures of them. I hid from my children and looked: the enemy soldiers were round, oval, elliptical, square, white, red, pink, and multicolored, so cute, in fact, that you could barely blame yourself for wanting to abuse them. They winked like aliens, but not like Russians, Japanese, Koreans, Mexicans, and all the other enemies we used to have. Clever little buggers! Instead of helmets they wore caps. Instead of rifles to kill you they carried charges that made you feel good. Clearly, this is guerrilla war: the enemy is encapsulated! Everything in a war is propaganda, so let's get rid of the doctors, too. The line dividing legal and illegal drugs is too subtle in these times of grave national danger.

Get Your *Pravda!*
Special Opium Issue!

P   *ravda* in English! It hit the newsstands last week and news-
     boys all over America are already learning to chant:
"EXTRA! PRAVDA! THE TRUTH IN ENGLISH!" Boy oh boy!
Pravda, the newspaper with more words per square inch than the
condensed *Oxford English Dictionary*! No banter! No bad news!
No news at all, in fact!

When I was growing up we had *Scânteia*, the Romanian clone
of *Pravda*. The front page is what people used to cure their in-
somnia. One look at it and you'd be snoring where you stood.
You had to be careful not to look at it till nighttime, because its
effect was swift. It was the reason why everywhere in Romania,
like everywhere in the Soviet Union, the populace was asleep
and snoring. People snoring at their desks, bent over assembly
lines, at public meetings, in long lines at the grocery stores. The
narcotic effect of these papers was attributed to certain recurring
words and phrases in their pages, such as *productivity*, *five-year
plan*, *strides forward*, *progress*, and *dialectical*. These in various
combinations were, are, and perhaps forever will be the active
ingredients of this powerful opiate.

All the people in America who have been complaining that
the news is always bad now have an alternative. The news is not
bad in *Pravda*. In *Pravda* only good things happen: the bad things
are only hypothetical. Imperialists, capitalists, oligarchists,
revisionists, Trotskyists—they are mentioned as bad but abstract.
Also, for those sick of advertising, *Pravda* offers a dark oasis of
respite: there are no ads. There aren't even pictures. The march-
ing forward (always forward!) columns of print are almost solid
black. They remind me of the page of a certain manuscript I once
saw. It had been written by an inmate of a Soviet prison camp,
who had only this one sheet of paper. He wrote a whole novel

on it. The words were so crowded that to the untrained eye the page looked like a solid block of darkness. To the discerning eye, however, worlds would unfold.

Likewise, if one can only keep one's discerning eyes open, worlds will unfold in *Pravda*. They will be rosy, rainbow-hued, and magical, and the people in them, those who aren't asleep, will be bent over their little sheets of paper, composing novels hiding worlds.

Soviet Life

aking a cue from the *Reader's Digest* Sweepstakes, *Soviet Life* magazine is flooding the mailboxes of America. "12 Big Issues for $9.95: A *Savings* of $11.05 off the Regular Price!" Wow! I remember seeing stacks of *Soviet Life* for ten cents each in the dusty bargain bin of my local socialist bookstore for years. I'd bought a few to cut up and make collages from, but the invariably smiling faces and fuzzily photographed tractors eventually bored even my scissors. But now, with glasnost and all, we might get something slicker. Clearly, though, the advertising has a way to go. A savings of $11.05? That's as un-American a number as you'll ever see: nobody cares about .05 here. The American fraction is .99. But no quibbling with small things—if you subscribe, you can win, quote, "one of two all-expenses-paid trips to the Soviet Union." That'll show that lousy million from *Reader's Digest*! You can also, believe it or not, get a square mile of Russia for one-tenth of a cent, or so I gather from this claim: "What country occupies 8.6 million square miles—nearly 15% of the earth's dry land—and is now waiting for you to get it . . . for just 83 cents a month?" I know we got a good deal on Alaska, but *this* is unbelievable.

The ad goes on to promise that *Soviet Life* will "whet your desire" to know the country better. I have heard of having one's appetite whetted, but *desire*? Are they one and the same in Russia? A little later we read an extraordinary admission, clearly an expression of glasnost: "Learn how the Soviet Union copes with worldwide problems such as environmental protection and overcrowding." I realize that "environmental protection" is a "problem" for every government, but a little bureaucratic cover-up usually takes care of that just fine.

My letter from *Soviet Life* is signed by Vladimir Belyakov, editor-in-chief. It is my guess that Mr. Belyakov is either the old editor with a glasnost fire under his seat or a new editor with a Madison Avenue training video in his office. In today's *Soviet Life* , the people are still hopelessly smiling, and still look cut out and pasted together. But the tractors aren't too fuzzy.

Agora: The Country of Exile

A *gora* is a little magazine of Romanian culture in exile. Its distinguished board includes Eugène Ionesco and Monica Lovinescu, but also other well-known East European writers, Josef Skvorecky and Geza Szöcs among them. Like other publications by language-sick refugees in the West, it wallows in the pleasures of its forsaken sounds. Some of its contributors have been away a long time. Their native tongue is like a whispering shrine carefully tended at the center of a noisy and alien house. Its flame flickers, threatening to go out at any moment, only to flare back up in the presence of the newer arrivals in whom the language still burns brightly.

Culture is maintained and made in a state of feverish contagion whose symptoms include some guilt and bitterness, certainly despair and longing, but also daring and faith in the ability to make worldwide sense. While *Agora* is the body in which the illness of exile rages, it attempts to say something of importance to the host culture as well. It tells it that to be in exile from Romania these days is to be witness to a new measure of space, time, and culture. Less than a decade ago, Romania was still accessible. Today it has dropped from the map of the world. Its economy is in shambles, there is a permanent food shortage, the lights go out in the evening, the mad dictator builds monuments to himself on the sites of old churches. If you're looking for the nineteenth century, a businessman remarked, this will soon be the place.

Maintaining the integrity of the culture under these circumstances becomes a great necessity. The task is immense, but *Agora*'s editor, Dorin Tudoran, seems equal to it. Tudoran was once Romania's best-known dissident, and the edge of his anger remains sharp. The urgency of his task rings through the texts of his contributors, directly or indirectly. Historical and critical essays unfold under this weighty light. The question of how to continue existing as a Romanian in exile occupies Petru Popescu, who writes that the expatriate Romanian, once a rarity, is now commonplace. You can hear Romanian spoken on the streets of Los Angeles. Living abroad, he concludes, has become natural for Romanians. What then remains of this barely comprehensible place in a world that is rapidly changing? *Agora*, a little literary magazine for exiles forging themselves a home from a language under pressure, a secret language.

Our century's literature, its culture perhaps, is mostly the work of exiles. Since World War I the West has been a landing strip for people fleeing history. The overcrowded country of exile has just made room for the keening of yet another generation.

Don't Cry for Me, Transylvania

There is big news from Transylvania, where I was born: the government is discouraging the Pan Am Dracula Tour. This is the tour, in case you're not familiar with the only folklore our two cultures share, set up to bring dollars to Romania, where Transylvania is. Romania is one of those sad workers' paradises where everybody's starving to death. Dracula has been good business, but suddenly the government's discouraging tourists. The problem is T-shirts. The tourists not only wear them, they want to buy them. "We know we could make a lot of money that way," said a Romanian official to an American reporter, "but we just can`t bring ourselves to sell our country so cheaply." He loosened his tie as he spoke, as if going to bare his naked chest to underline his point: T-shirts are not well regarded in this workers' paradise. In Romania, as in the Soviet Union, the business suit is the uniform of choice. A communist bureaucrat would rather starve in a suit than feast in a T-shirt. There is a grandeur in that. You may recall that Dracula himself is always impeccably dressed prior to slurping up virgin blood. "I would rather live in the basement of a palace than live in the best rooms of a slum," says an old Transylvanian proverb.

It is ironic, though not surprising, that it falls to the communist countries to keep up the capitalist image. A few years ago when long hair was the enemy, Romanians vigorously hounded anyone with hair out of the ordinary. By comparison, the rednecks of America treated hippies with kid gloves. There can be only one explanation: Henry Ford, not Karl Marx, is responsible for communism. Are T-shirts allowed in Greenfield Village, the Henry Ford Museum? Is long hair allowed in Disneyland? Of course, but only after a long struggle. In Transylvania, on the other hand, the line is drawn. Only business suits can enter. Henry Ford is immortal here; he swings down the assembly line of ages to instill propriety in tourists.

Swallowing the Boss

M y son says that T-shirts with the Coca-Cola company logo are all the rage now. They cost upwards of forty dollars each and the youth of America is tripping over itself to get into them. Hallelujah! Advertising has reached critical mass at long last: the ads no longer come just from that yonder TV set, they also come right on up from inside ourselves. Imagine being a sandwich man for a big corporation without being paid for it! Coca-Cola now has attained the status of apple pie in the Pantheon of Schlock, right alongside Mother and Country. When the youth of America is finally all clad in corporation logos, you may no more question those corporations than you can apple pie, Mother, or Country. Even now, it would take something like Freud, anarchy, and Snow White's stepmother to sow the seeds of doubt about Coke.

A few years back I made fun of personalized license plates and T-shirts sporting one-liners that synthetically expressed the owner's philosophy. Those things now seem to belong to an era of innocence, a long-gone age of rugged individualism. KISS ME, I'M IRISH, or Ph.D. FROM THE SCHOOL OF HARD KNOCKS are fierce expressions of difference compared to sporting a company logo. The one-liners of yore are to the logos of now what Marcel Proust is to the adventures of Garfield.

There is a dark side to this business, however, and it has to do with advertising's ability to turn a person against himself. All ads are made to persuade you to purchase something you might not otherwise consider. When you are so persuaded that you are willing to pay money to become an ad yourself, you may be acting exactly like the victim who enthusiastically takes on the oppressor's point of view.

In Louisiana recently, we had the dubious honor of leading the nation in unemployment. The ultimate obscenity I can conceive of is an out-of-work Coca-Cola bottler walking around in a T-shirt with the company logo. Ultimate chic: devotion to the whip.

The Eyes Have It

TV shopping is here. A luscious-looking ham slides into view. All you have to do is call. All day long you sit in an armchair and watch things you might want to buy. The trouble is that you're shopping only with your eyes and your ears. You're not shopping with your fingertips. Your nose has no say in it. You can't put a potential purchase to your cheek to see how it feels. The eyes have it. The ears got it. Here, as in most everything else in this world, sight and sound have taken over. The other senses are in exile. The nose, running out of things to smell, has begun to shrink. Once a glorious schnozzle, now a mere button nose, it will soon be no more. The vast tactile sea that used to cover your skin and peak in your fingertips is drying up. Your taste buds will soon abandon your tongue like little migrating birds, leaving it good only for wagging. Your cravings, unchecked by the play of your senses, will grow enormous. The eyes and ears set no limits to your desires. They send images and whispers directly to the pleasure centers.

It seems that the market ought to be overjoyed by its triumph. But it is not. People are buying everything too fast. Production can't keep up with demand. A subtle advertising campaign has been launched. It tries to aim products only at certain people. It tries to create a type of consumer, in order to limit demand. In so doing, it creates new social distinctions, false social classes whose differences are based not on wealth or birth but on the consumption of certain products. Very soon, you'll have to earn the right to buy certain exclusive products. "Are you worthy of Gag Cola?" might read a future ad campaign. "If you are sick or ugly, don't bother asking!" Eventually, there will be a million consumer classes. Each of us will have a pocket crave-reader. If you want something, it will compute the quantity of advertising you have absorbed about the product to see if you are worthy of it. It will calculate how much you can afford to spend and even direct you to the nearest place to satisfy your craving. If, however, it finds that your craving exceeds your bank balance, it will calculate how much you are likely to earn in the future. And if you appear unable to support a continued desire for the product—it terminates you.

In the future, we will all have smooth heads without mouths or noses. We will have huge ears and eyes and will all be aristocrats ready to die for what we want.

Instant Traditions

E very year Christmas gets bigger. It looms at the end of the year like a large black hole of capitalism ready to suck you by your credit line straight into nothingness. A few years ago, you gave the kids a toy each and they hugged you. Now they want cars, computers, and ski vacations and they make your life miserable if you can't afford them.

Like every other so-called tradition of late-twentieth-century America, Christmas is anything but. Tradition, the way my pal Laura puts it, is just a marketing strategy. "Let's create a new tradition," cry the advertisers, and there we are, newly traditionalized under a river of turkeys. The Thanksgiving turkey was the brainchild of a nineteenth-century woman's magazine, a brainchild then co-opted by entrepreneurial bird growers. Next week it will, no doubt, be time for a revolution against the "old" tradition because swan farmers will have somehow edged out the turkey industry. Watch what happens to "tradition" when it no longer suits the needs of the market. Capitalism is fundamentally against tradition because tradition implies loyalty to something in the past and if it's past it means you already bought it. Capitalism cares only for the future, for what you're going to buy tomorrow.

Capitalism is, in fact, against the very backbone of tradition, the family. Families aren't good buyers: several people use one refrigerator, one stove, and one gravy boat. Singles, on the other hand, each use a refrigerator, stove, etc. Divorce is good for capitalism. Furthermore, if the single person can be divided and buy something for different aspects of his or her personality, like a different color refrigerator for each day and each mood, then so much the better. Schizophrenia is the ultimate result of a healthy market.

A few human-based festivities survive here and there, growing like wild grass between the cracks in the pavement of modern life. There is not much money in Halloween, for instance, and it has begun to rival Christmas as the country's greatest holiday. Nor is there much commerce associated with Mardi Gras, though there is a great flurry of social activity. What these two venerable traditions have in common is the use of masks to escape our everyday persons. Our everyday persons are shoppers. We are condemned by our dailiness to an endless merry-go-round of working and buying. Not so at Halloween or Mardi Gras, when we give up our treadmill identities for those of fantastic beings that exist outside time. Dracula doesn't shop. He just takes what he needs. Nor are warlocks, witches, and angels much concerned with the mechanics of our consumer economy. Immortality means not having to buy or sell, but rather to fly, or prowl, or slink, or leap. There are no stores in the imagination, but the market would dearly love to put some there. In fact, I'll bet my bat wings that someone's somewhere working on a mid-flight mall for vampires.

But autumn is past, alas. The unappeasable maw of winter opens wide as I hide from my children to write this. OK, kids, things are not what they seem. This is not the Christmas of your childhood that you were once so fond of. This is different. This is Christmas in a world populated by heavily indebted schizophrenics going to pieces as we speak, each piece with its own credit card. Let us gather these fragments of ourselves for a moment, and, as we raise glasses to our equally fragmented loved ones around a Christmas tree obscured by a mountain of gifts, let us remember tradition. Unfortunately, capitalism's against memory too, because remembering has loyalty as a by-product, and being loyal to your memories means not living in the present which means not buying.

What were we supposed to remember anyway?

In the True Church

I don't often go to church but when I do, I go to the real one: I turn on "The Price Is Right." That's the original American church and I like my things basic. Lately, however, this bastion of commodity worship is being displaced by "Wheel of Fortune." Even "60 Minutes," *that* bastion of serious journalism, did a piece on Pat Sajak and Vanna White, calling them, respectively, the "Wonderbread" and "Garbo" of prime-time TV. Mr. Wonderbread's specialty is blandness, while Vanna's is turning letters over. I had thought that their appeal, just like that of "60 Minutes," is to that endearing quality of the eighties to be as boring as possible, which leads directly to the army and the shopping mall, but upon reflection I decided that this is actually not the case. I had also thought that Vanna was the ultimate TV creature, a Dada artist who does not speak but methodically destroys language by revealing clichés letter by letter, day after day, year after year.

This is somewhat the case, but not the main one. At issue is not their quality but religious competition between the old American Church of the Price Is Right and the new Church of the Wheel. In the old church, there are rather large prizes given away after a few ritualistic parlor games, mostly to large people who look like they deserve them, just as cripples deserve to be healed in other churches. In the Church of the Wheel the prizes are meager and the prices outrageous: there is a $3,000 vacation to a New Orleans flophouse, $1,000 ceramic dogs, $500 bookends. These prices have not arrived yet in the real world; they are the prices of the future. And herein lies the meaning of the

Wheel: it is preparing us for an inflated future in which bad taste at outrageous prices will be the new sacrament. Say goodbye to the solid middle-class sacraments of refrigerators and washing machines of "The Price Is Right." Say hello to the ceramic dogs and geriatric cruises of "Wheel of Fortune."

If you're lucky.

"Miami Vice" and the
New Cult of the "Real"

"**M**iami Vice" took on art the other night and added a new dimension to the hall of mirrors that is the deranged mind of television. An artist/filmmaker makes a "snuff" movie, and Tubbs and Crockett attempt to find out whether a girl in the movie was actually killed. The artist is exploiting the public's confusion between what's real and what's art and gives a speech to that effect on a TV monitor that our erstwhile detectives watch while we watch them on TV. So far nothing unusual: TV is enamored of itself and it is only the costly conceit of maintaining the illusion of the "real" that keeps TV from being entirely and overtly self-referential.

Crockett is never taken in by this "illusion/reality" stuff the artist spouts because he is, you see, a "real" man. He forges ahead and discovers that the murder has indeed been committed. But it is impossible to indict the artist because the law is too unsubtle to distinguish reality from illusion. And so Crockett, the dispenser of justice, goes alone to see the artist. "So you think violence is attractive?" he says. Then he proceeds to beat the hell out of the trickster for confusing things. This beating, which is meant to condemn violence, is a highly satisfactory climax to the dilemma posed by art. The enlightened viewer now has a handle on how to deal with the confusion between life and art—learned from TV.

Crockett, of course, has been so successful at obliterating the distinction between life and art that his conceit is not even in question. His is an attack on "high art," on those things that escape the increasing control of television over the passage between reality and illusion. Artists like that, he suggests, are effete snobs who need a good beating. They go about confusing the common man, who knows for himself what's real and what's not. He saw it on TV. If there is anybody out there who doesn't recognize this as classic fascist ideology, I will give him or her my TV set. Meanwhile, I watch. Gotta keep track of the latest in ideological prompting.

A Big Moment

I ncidents that trigger history are rare and far between, thank God. Some of them are obvious, even loud, like the shot that killed Archduke Ferdinand at Sarajevo and was instantly credited with starting World War I. Others are not so obvious as they occur, but in retrospect garner full historical-trigger status, like the sinking of the *Titanic*. An entire era, the great age of the luxury liner, was later seen to have sunk with that ship. Other incidents are more elusive yet, and may never float fully into symbolic recognition. The recent sale of van Gogh's painting "Irises" for nearly $54,000,000 is one of these.

Van Gogh painted his "Irises" when he was a patient at the insane asylum at Saint-Rémy-en-Provence. It was his period of most intense suffering and utmost subjectivity. He painted what came uniquely from his own psyche, true expressionism that made his fellow post-Impressionists look, by comparison, like photojournalists. Money, the objective standard, was van Gogh's chief enemy. The only reason we have his great letters on painting is because he wrote them to his brother Theo begging for money for paint. "Dear Theo," he writes on 3 September 1882, "One thing I want to call your attention to, as being of importance. Would it be possible to get colors, panels, brushes, etc., *wholesale*? Now I have to pay the retail price. . . . If so, I think it would be much cheaper to buy white, ocher, sienna, for instance, wholesale, and then we could arrange about the money. It would of course be much cheaper. Think it over." And whether Theo did or not, van Gogh does bring it up over and over, and then feels guilty for burdening his brother. "Good painting," he continues, "does not depend on using much color, but in order to paint a ground forcefully, or to keep a sky clear, one must sometimes not spare the tube."

When he dared to think about his audience, van Gogh placed

it in the future. The future did more than provide him with an audience; it transformed his subjectivity into a new objective standard. When "Irises" sold for more money than had ever been paid for an art object, the utmost subjectivity met the utmost objectivity, and a historical moment occurred. The fevered impressions of a madman met the sober calculations of a great fortune. Van Gogh's power came from his unconscious; the money used to buy his work was entirely the result of conscious calculation and deliberation. The meeting of the two is not history that yields immediate access. The point is obscure. It may even mean the exact opposite of what it *seems* to mean, namely, that it is money, our so-called objective standard, that is truly subjective—a matter of tenuous agreement—and art, the so-called subjective world, is the way things really are. In that case, individual expression in its most extreme subjective form is the true currency, while money, bound by so many extraneous ponderables, is a mere illusion.

At their extremes, opposites tend to become each other. When the auctioneer's gavel came down on van Gogh's "Irises," an irreversible reversion occurred. Art became money and money became what used to be art. The new money, art, will be a wildly fluctuating medium of exchange. It will mean one thing to one person and another to another. Welcome to the new barter economy! It will confuse and disrupt all the workers of the world who expect uniform pay for regular work. This economy will be based on sleight of hand and gimmickry or, at times, even originality and quirkiness. It will not be hard, for instance, to convince you to exchange a perfectly good car for my fevered imaginings. I will just remind you of "Irises." That is all fine by me, because I am an artist, but I cringe to think of the masses fooled into watching TV and working regular jobs. For them, it will seem like the end of the world. Some will join the ranks of strict fundamentalism in order to give their lives an unchanging meaning. Others will become artists, maybe even great artists, or great scam artists.

The sale of van Gogh's "Irises" signifies the end of the second industrial age.

Why Art?

Once in a while someone goes bonkers and heads for art with a hammer. It used to be statues the vandals were after, but recently a man in London fired a shotgun blast at a drawing by Leonardo, thereby changing both the object and the intensity of anti-art sentiment.

What moves these vandals? In the past century, both pro- and anti-lust forces castrated Greek and Roman statues. That was a personal and rather intimate form of vandalism. Later on, Picasso took Renoir's women and exploded them into cubes—a subtle act of vandalism that changed art forever. By the time Marcel Duchamp painted a mustache on the Mona Lisa, vandalism was the new philosophy of art. Picasso didn't, of course, blow up the actual Renoirs, nor did Duchamp paint over the original Mona Lisa, but some people are more literal-minded than they. Still, what was the man with the shotgun in London *really* aiming at? Had he perhaps had some revelation of a great evil embodied in art? Perhaps he was worried about inflation and its relation to the human soul.

When a painting by van Gogh goes for some $54,000,000, one can't help wondering at the great gap between the living and the dead. A middle-class man in an industrially developed country is worth about $600,000 in insurance. The difference between him and "Irises" is $53,400,000, which is either the price of publicity or the price of a nameless something we don't quite understand. It is, in any case, a hefty increase over the value of art in other times, when value equaled use and the object was only as good as the function it served.

Can this large sum reflect the absolute power of advertising over the acts of basic life? The public act gone haywire? Are we being extorted in order to become spectators of the machine that extorts us? Has the religion of art joined with militarism to empty first our pockets, then our souls? So here comes this man, tormented by these and other questions, carrying a shotgun. A hammer may have been sufficient when the price was in the thousands. Millions call for firepower.

The One-Thing-Only Store

I went to an art show where the gallery owner showed only things he made himself. He wasn't in the least embarrassed. I remember a similar shop in California, in Tiburon, where the proprietor, an old Chinese watercolorist, sold only his own work. There must have been a time, before the advent of the modern entrepreneur, when such a thing was common. You went into a store because all the chairs there were made by one man. Of course, he also fixed chairs. The same went for the dressmaker. And the watchmaker. Come to think of it, the idea of a store with more than one man's work for sale must be quite recent.

I think that things have gotten out of hand. There are just too many things by too many people all in one place. I would like to open a bookstore that sells only my own books. People could come in, browse, buy or not buy, but at least they'd know what they were getting into. If they liked my stuff, they'd be back. The place would be a critical clearinghouse as well; there is no telling the kind of good advice I'd pick up. The customers could write their comments in a big fat book that could then be published as a separate volume and sold in the store. Comments would then be added about this book, and a new book made of them. And so on until the place is filled to bursting by the expanding *oeuvre* that would be a collaboration between myself and my readers.

I bet that's how reputations were made in the old days. After all, what is there to do in a store that sells only one thing—a chair, for example—once that thing is viewed? Make conversation with the proprietor, of course. Talk about the chair, about the materials it's made from, maybe even sit in it, spend more and more time in the shop. Clearly, the old times were not very efficient. All that talk made for fewer chairs. Nowadays we've put more things in that place formerly occupied by talk. Instead of opening our mouths to consider, we furrow our brows to inwardly count, calculate, try to decide.

I prefer getting it over with, then paying some attention to how such a thing came to be, and how it, not to mention the world, can be made better, and so on and so on.

My Brush with Hollywood

I've had my brush with Hollywood. A big producer called me. "Howdja like to do a daily syndicated TV show?" he asked.

"Sure," I said. I saw the whirlpool bath, sauna, mountaintop retreat, and Mercedes-Benz before he finished the sentence.

"I heard you on the radio today. I'd like to see some scripts and hear a tape."

Sho' thing, boss man. I wrapped up a book and a tape and express-mailed them. Yes, I hate TV. I'm the one who calls it the idiot box and worse. On the other hand, said I to myself, if I can say on TV the same things I say on radio, what's the difference? I'll put on a clean shirt and a good pair of pants. It's not the end of the world. I'll comb my hair. I can still call TV the idiot box on TV.

Two days after sending the book and the tape, I started to fidget. TV is the *enemy*. It has rendered us moronic from sea to shining sea. Maybe I was selling too cheap. What avails a man a Mercedes-Benz if he's bought it with his soul? The world's *full* of soulless guys in Mercedeses. I was standing firm when at last the phone call came.

"I *like* these," the man said, "but they seem . . . literary. Doncha have anything about Thanksgiving, Christmas, and other American foibles?"

"If they're written down, they're literary," I said. "When they're on tape, they're not. They won't be so literary on TV."

He said he'd mull it over.

After he hung up, I shook my head for shame. Was there no limit to the things I'd do for a hot tub? Let's see. I wouldn't sell my mother. I wouldn't do advertising. I wouldn't work for the Pentagon. I wouldn't publish in *The New Yorker*. I wouldn't buy

Krugerrands. I wouldn't eat swan. My list was no longer than that when the phone rang again. It was Hollywood.

"I'm sorry," said Hollywood, "but your material is too elevated for TV."

Phew! Of course! How did I ever think for a moment otherwise?

"That's all right," I said. "I was just about to call to say that I've decided not to do it."

There was genuine surprise at the other end. "No?" he said.

"Well, unless I could do exactly what I *do* . . . and provided, of course, that . . ."

I nauseated myself. Was there no end to the greedy tapeworm in my breast? I unplugged the phone and took a vow of silence.

Barge: The Movie

*B*arge: *The Movie*, a made-for-TV film starring Sylvester Stallone, will air on Father's Day. This is a thoughtful and compelling drama that examines the chief question of *fin de siècle* capitalism: "Where do I put my garbage?"

After failing to put their garbage in places traditionally designated as the garbage dumps of the nation and the world, such as Louisiana and Mexico, the garbage producers are dramatically faced by their own product. Shortly after the opening credits, one of the crewmen, who is from Louisiana, says, "Pinch da tails an' suck da heads! We're bottom feeders, heck!" His little joke will come to haunt him as the barge begins its hapless journey around the world, shunned by everyone like B. Traven's *Death Ship* and causing horror and dismay like *The Flying Dutchman*.

Barge: The Movie would be nothing without the sensitively portrayed relationships on board. As the journey enters its second week, the land-forsaken crewmen have lost all their appetite. Stallone, in one of his rare appearances as a sensitive human being, urges his shipmates to eat. The alternative is too horrifying to contemplate. "Eat da grub!" he hollers. "Da wind's gonna change!"

But the wind *doesn't* change and the atmosphere aboard the barge becomes laden with violence and questions. When one of the crewmen goes mad and wildly beseeches God to finish him off, Stallone turns equally wild and metaphysical. He strikes the fallen man with his fist and says, "God didn't make da garbage! People made it!" He continues to beat the enfeebled crewman senseless while asking God a series of poignant questions about His relationship to the human race and the relationship of the human race to garbage. As the barge floats past cities and countries on its nightmare journey, we feel the chill of the future. The final note is struck by Stallone staring longingly at the stars, which to him look clean and unspoiled in their tiny places in heaven.

Barge: The Movie is a series pilot. This fall it becomes an unwanted but inevitable weekly drama, floating through our TVs for God knows how many seasons.

Downriver

T he word's not good from downriver. It's no fun waiting for that big mess from Ohio to float down to us. How long will it take? Three weeks? Four months? However long, it doesn't change the universal law: we folks downriver are forever waiting for whatever folks upriver will send us. Every glass of water in New Orleans, goes the old saw, has already been drunk six times. Of course, the trouble's not all from upriver. We do our best to poison our own water: we dump radioactive runoff from gypsum into it, pump petrochemical by-products and empty our toilets into it, too. An overworked filter is supposed to take out all the bad chemicals. But then—radioactivity isn't a chemical. Every few months a new report tells us how vile our water is. As if the highest rates of liver and pancreas cancer in the nation weren't enough.

No Louisianan in his right mind drinks the river water, unless he's poor, and the poor are, obviously, not in their right minds since they are poor. As a mayoral candidate put it during the debates: "Folks uptown drink Kentwood, folks downtown get cancer." Guess who lives downtown? Downtown, downriver, downtrodden, and just plain *down*: all these words apply to the riverwater drinkers around here.

A great many of us don't drink water at all. The many festivals we have here—including Mardi Gras—were created as excuses not to. Nevertheless, there comes that time in the middle of the night when you stumble into the kitchen to fetch yourself a glass from the faucet before you're thinking clearly. You hold it in your sleepy hand, and just as you're about to bring it to your lips, it begins to glow—and hum! Mutated microorganisms come to life with an eerie luminescence while trace minerals from every discarded chemical by-product start singing softly. A cobalt blue radioactive light of indefinite source plays softly over the whole show. "Drink us," the horrors croon, looking quite beautiful in their man-begotten glow, "and you can be just like us!" And you do, because it's late, and you're thirsty, and you think it's all a bad dream. But it's not: it's the middle of the night three months from now and the mess from Ohio has finally arrived!

Casinos

Casino gambling's the issue in Dixie, and everybody, including the governor, is betting on it. Gambling featured prominently in a recent investigation into the man's personal finances. He barely managed to wiggle out of it without an indictment. It seems he liked to owe millions to guys from out of state who knew him under Chinese pseudonyms. He paid back some of it with suitcases full of cash. Now that he's almost innocent, our leader would like to gamble at home. New Orleans is famous for other borderline fun, stuff like Mardi Gras and all-night bars, so why not gambling? It's part of the lore, after all. Mark Twain himself spent many smoky nights in gambling dens down here. There are arguments back and forth. People against it cite corruption and crime. People for it cite increased revenue and more jobs. Those are all good arguments, but I have my own take on casinos. It's born of experience.

I once badly needed a quick hundred bucks. With the four hundred already in my checking account, that would cover the rent and one-month deposit on a great new apartment I'd been offered—with only twenty-four hours to respond. Instead of borrowing the money, I decided I'd win it in Reno. I took a one-way trip on a plane from San Francisco—eighteen bucks—and got to Reno just in time for a gorgeous sunset. I plunked down a C note on blackjack and doubled it. I let it ride and doubled that. Then I doubled *that*. I now had eight hundred bucks and the thought came to me that I could luxuriate in a room upstairs, take a bubble bath, drink a bottle of good champagne, take in a show, go home, and *still* have enough dough for the new joint. But I had a demon now. *Only once more*, a voice whispered.

Come the glorious sunrise, I rose from the gaming table with a stiff back. I had a sweaty quarter in my hand. It was going to be a crisp, blue, fresh mountain day. I stood looking for a while from a bridge at the turbulent Truckee River and thought how lucky I was to be poor, free, and alive in God's world. I hitched a ride back to the city with a guy who bought me a hamburger and some fries. Stayed on in the old apartment. Resolved never to gamble. It's an easy resolution to keep, with the casinos way out there in Jersey and Nevada. I don't know about having them right next door.

Oil and the Sin Tax

T he dropping price of oil is bad news in Louisiana. The rest of the world may be imagining a new age of affluence just around the corner, but down here we're looking mournfully at the future. Just like the grasshopper in Aesop's famous fable, Louisiana wishes that it had been singing "God Bless the Child That's Got Its Own" instead of "Laissez les bon temps rouler." Letting the rest of the world pay your bills is OK if you plan to die young, but Louisiana doesn't. Even if the prices weren't dropping, oil is on its way out, and oil companies, never known for their altruism despite their liking for the ballet, aren't going to stick around to see what happens. They'll leave behind a chemical sewer filled with toxic waste and an unemployment rate that will make Haiti look good.

Our multiply indicted governor is a symbol of the age just past: a charming, loudmouth megalomaniac with instant solutions to everything. While the legislature is talking about a 20 percent across-the-board cut in education spending—and this in a state that already has the most bankrupt education system in the country—the governor talks gambling as the cure to all evils. The governor isn't the only dreamer around. The Church recommends new sin taxes on cigarettes and liquor instead. Meanwhile, we have no property taxes, and a recent proposal to levy $50 annually for every $100,000 home has little chance of making it.

This peculiar mix of backwardness and upside-down priorities is matched only by an even more peculiar mix of bravado and hype. The highly vocal locals imagine that they can weather anything if only nobody bothers them to take part in the political process. Years of corruption and neglect have made cynics of them all. And Lord knows that voodoo isn't going to save us.

A Third World country is rapidly emerging from inside the United States. Some say that, psychologically, Louisiana has always been one. Instead of taxing liquor, cigarettes, and houses, let's start taxing guns and baloney. Everybody'll soon be using the several guns they already own to get their food in the swamps, and they'll be talking a lot less baloney while they wait for it to come within firing range.

Guns and baloney. Get ready, Louisiana.

Kafka's Hell

N o, I say. No. Don't give it to them, no matter how much they beg for it. First it was ten cents. Then it was thirteen. Then it was fifteen, eighteen, twenty, twenty-two. Now it is twenty-five. They *want* twenty-seven. First they cried *Poverty*! and we believed them. Now they cry *Computers*! and we believe them still. I say *Basta*! The Post Office shouldn't get a penny until they deliver our letters.

Where is my letter from Allan, mailed in Minneapolis two weeks ago? Where is my note from Addy, mailed in Baton Rouge ten days ago? Where is my book from Jessica, mailed three weeks ago? What happened to my rent check, mailed across town eight days ago? Why did my letters to Keith and to John come back although they were addressed correctly? Where are the mailmen of yesteryear? Where are the uncomputerized eyes of real people who know the town and will bring me my letters even when the ZIP code is wrong? It's not more computers the Post Office needs, but more humans, and fewer lazy ones. Why are the lines there always a mile long? Who sits in the back there with my mail, reading it under fluorescent lamps? Who rips open my packages so that they come to me torn and spilled?

Who raised the newspaper rates so high that it now costs me more to mail my magazine than it does to print it? Who is it who raises the price for freedom of speech? Where are the good men and women who once could deliver a letter for you with only a name and a city written on it? *Where are the mailmen of yesteryear*? Bring back the people, I say; chuck the machines! We don't need any more machines. Under our feet, behind our backs, over our heads all there are are machines. And we pay and pay for them, even as they throw us in the dead letter file, the dead letter office where all humans will soon come to reside. And there, there maybe are all the letters not delivered, not processed, un-ZIP-coded, shredded, and disappeared.

My favorite book title is that of a poetry collection by Ted Berrigan called *Nothing for You*. I used to think it was a warning to the reader not to identify too strongly with the poet's material, but then Ted set me straight: "That's what the mailman says when you've been waiting for him all day. 'Nothing for you.'" Well, from now on, it's nothing for the mailman. I want to read my mail *now*—and until I do, not another penny, I say. Not another cent for Kafka's machine hell. Bring back the mailmen of yesteryear.

Letters

My mail is a distinct and precious part of my life, like the house I live in, or my adolescence, or an inner organ, say, a kidney. Ever since I can remember, the arrival of the postman was what made the day complete. It's as if there is a hole in me and it can only be filled by letters. If there aren't enough, the hole cries for satisfaction and causes imbalance in the rest of me. As I get older, the hole gets bigger. The more mail I get, the more it demands.

Yes, mail is a sickness with me. I blame it all on my father, who never wrote to me. One summer when I was about ten and suffering at some summer camp, he came to visit and gave me a wad of money. There was nothing to buy there, and there was also no toilet paper. After he left I used the money. It is to that sad incident that I trace both my disregard for common currency and my mania for mail. Had he written me a few personal words instead of giving me money, which everybody can read, I might have turned out less voracious. As it is, I'd trade all the money in the world for an intimate note. For me, the true currency is the words that people say only to each other.

There are, of course, varying levels of intimacy in my post. I get an awful lot of letters from people who want something from me because they're under the mistaken impression that I'm famous. Actually, I have no "in" with the powers. They weaken when I speak. And then there are fan letters, those lovely white-winged birds that alight softly on my desk. Once in a while among them there squats a vulture or a bat, but they are mostly snowy swans and doves, occasionally a crane or a pelican. And then there are the letters from my friends. These are the ones that truly appease that hungry hole inside me. *Dearest whomever. It's been a long time. Wish you were here.*

New Concepts in Grazing

I went grazing in a new super-duper yuppie market with a friend of mine who is the founder of Market Grazers of America. Before we started to graze ourselves, he pointed out to me the various herds of grazers in the various sections. There were a couple in the fruit section popping grapes and figs while secreting two kumquats each in overextended cheeks. We followed two old sisters in Victorian ruffles through the salad bar and saw them roll carrot strips elegantly down their gullets, chased by dainty radishes and translucent cuke slices. Two large lunch-hour stockbrokers or stockjobbers were doing sausages and chicken wings from off the hot rotisserie. Each took a turn covering for the other until they took enough turns to empty the case. A couple of foreigners were doing cheeses and rolls. Two Edams and a block of feta got grazed right out of an imported-cheese pyramid.

The odd thing was that, even as we watched the grazers at work, various free samples were being distributed throughout the store, things like salsa on crackers and smoked turkey beaks, but the grazers weren't taking any. True grazers, my friend told me, pay no attention to free samples. They are outlaws and artists, and art makes high demands.

My friend, the spearhead of the MGA, has a weekend hobby too. He likes to raid his wealthy neighbors' garbage every Saturday. They throw away great stuff. The trick is never to let them come to visit; they might have a mental breakdown should they open the refrigerator. He has noticed that his own garbage is often raided by people from poorer neighborhoods which he makes a point of never visiting. In addition to his two hobbies, my friend also has a job. He works for the State Department. Based on his activities as a grazer and garbage raider in an upscale neighborhood, he has developed a new foreign policy concept. Open the borders, he says, and let Third World countries in for a whole week to raid our garbage and graze the supermarkets. They can take turns, and we won't have to put out a penny in foreign aid. He has the wholehearted support of the Bush administration.

When he told me this idea, I told him I needed a drink. We palmed ourselves a corkscrew and grazed the wine section, taking sips out of various bottles then putting them back on the shelf.

The Hidden Wealth

Saint Charles Avenue in New Orleans has to be the most charming boulevard in the world. Its tree-lined mansions tell lovely stories in the flower-festooned evenings. Some of these great houses blaze with light, and through their windows one glimpses elegant people under crystal chandeliers with leather-bound books in their hands and dreamy-eyed children fidgeting on piano stools before venerable ivories.

Others are ruined palaces, behind whose shuttered windows scions of old Southern aristocracy huddle, no doubt, before cold marble fireplaces, with nothing left but their pride and one or two battered first editions of *Gone with the Wind*.

And then there are the other sorts of mansion: stately Georgians or Victorians with well-tended gardens and freshly painted wrought iron fences. But these are dark and, unlike the others, appear neither boastful nor *desuète*. They are simply uninhabited. The invisible hands of an army of servants keep them prim and proper for their absent owners.

I stopped in front of one of these last evening, and as I slowly succumbed to the fragrant opiate of the well-kept but eerily deserted grounds, it struck me: *hidden wealth!* The gorgeous villa seducing me is somebody's hidden wealth! It perhaps belongs to Imelda Marcos. I remembered a story told me about a sheik who kept one of these houses but had never once seen it. How *many* of these beauties, I wondered, belong to Arab oil men? Half the avenue might, for all I know. And how many others *are* there, I thought, whose hidden wealth maintains large and lovely estate the world over, each inhabited by none but phantom servants?

I, who have never had any hidden wealth on account of the fact that I've always spent it before I could hide it, was reminded that only a little, a very little, of the world as we know it can claim ownership by those who inhabit it. The rest of it, the vast majority of it, belongs to hidden wealth.

Pope-amania

T he Pope is coming to New Orleans and the city is turning into the Vatican. Already, there are more Pope knickknack about than things in everyday use. And things in everyday use have taken on Pope features. The plastic spoons and forks at my favorite fast-food joint sport the Pope on their handles. Two out of three T-shirts on men *and* women have the Pope on 'em. On some he blesses, fingers outstretched over the tops of pious bosoms, on others he's a Popealope—Pope as Jackalope— or Cyclopope—Pope as Cyclope. The popular imagination loves a good Pope. At the outdoor taverns, the plebes are drinking from Pope mugs, fanning themselves with Pope fans, jingling Pope keychains and getting off beer tops with bottle-Popeners. Children are swinging Pope-on-a-rope and getting their mouths washed out with Pope soap. Business is booming at Popeye's, the chicken chain, which is really *Pope Eyes*, a fact that doesn't escape Baptists fearful of popish plots. Dandies protect their sports cars with screens featuring the blessing Pope. There are Pope-sicles in the mouths of babes and Pope-tarts in every toaster. My Pope candle from the all-night store says, "He come in the name of the Lord." I try not to burn it at both ends.

The menus of the Pope are in the paper, every one of them. For breakfast he'll have red beans and white rice, the papal colors. For lunch, fish, featured in the gospels. For dinner, wafers étouffés. The chefs are taking it easy on the cayenne so the Pope won't weep for the wrong reasons. Gotta save those tears for real stuff.

Some people will die of heat at the outdoor Mass, we are told Can there be a straighter road to heaven? The Pope is expected attract more visitors than Mardi Gras, but the town will smell like incense, not beer. Local socialites are turning Polish. The city has put up new palm trees at $110 a pop along the route of the Popemobile. They've also painted a big Pope hat on the Superdome. Pope scams have sprung up, including the sale of tickets to out-of-towners for the free Mass.

Protest artists who want a piece of the Pope aren't sure exactly what might work on this particular pontiff. Years ago a Surrealist painter attacked another Pope in Spain. The judge said Surrealism was a religion that obliged one to attack the Pope. They let the painter go. But this Pope's a modern poet, though not a Surrealist. In Nicaragua he scolded Ernesto Cardenal, another priest poet, for being a Sandinista. Maybe poetry, not politics, is this Pope's real battleground. Let's put some poetry on walls and buses and find out. If he fails to notice, we can keep up for the Republican convention, coming up next. Everybody knows how big Bush is on poetry!

Nonetheless, the pontiff nears. Raise high those Popeye's boxes!

The Mind Circus Is in Town

The thousands of booksellers and publishers of America are in New Orleans to do what we do so well here: party. Antoine's, the famous granddaddy of all New Orleans restaurants, has been booked to the gills all weekend. Music is rising from every nook and cranny of the French Quarter. At Storyville Alain Toussaint will entertain the nominees for the American Book Awards and their guests. At my own modest book party, Raphael Cruz will make sexy jazz. Wrapped in the peppery air of continuously sizzling blackened redfish and the sounds of boogie, the business of selling the products of America's mind goes on apace. But despite the festive air, the fruits of America's mind aren't what we might want them to be.

This year, as in recent years, the big books at the American booksellers' convention were not written by writers. Johnny Cash, Walter Cronkite, David Stockman, Carol Burnett, Beverly Sills, James Brown, and Princess Michael of Kent are the current big names. It is the fruits of *their* minds that America wants to sample. And it is at them, not at us, that the big publishers fling handfuls of cash.

There are long lines at the autograph booths, but don't look for real writers there either. The river of ink flowing out of America's mind is for the most part a cascade of cheap thrills. Romances are as big as ever, if not bigger. Harlequin's steamy soft-core for the fantasy-impaired rises on billboards from the convention floor. This circus is only mildly amusing. Serious literature hugs the corners of the room, the work, mostly, of small independent publishers.

New Orleans was once home to William Faulkner, Sherwood Anderson, F. Scott Fitzgerald, Tennessee Williams, William Burroughs, and others, who found the genteel decrepitude well suited to dreaming. The literary trappings of New Orleans are, to be sure, a great drawing card to writers and dreamers. Not long ago, John Kennedy Toole, who dreamed up *A Confederacy of Dunces*, committed suicide here when no big eastern publisher would touch his novel. The small press of the state university finally did the book, and posthumously Toole was awarded the Pulitzer Prize. Such ironies are lost under the fluorescent lights of the convention hall. New York, of course, is where the money is, and consequently the floor of the convention is laid out just like midtown Manhattan, a grid of squares. Up and down the avenues stroll the publishers' reps and bookstore owners. Almost naked muscle-boys tout the latest in beefcake calendars. A sequined and bikinied bimbo with a snake around her shoulders hands everyone a brochure. What's she selling? Snake oil, no doubt. Two pretty girls stand before a display of tapes of lullabies, a soothing new therapy for the harried victims of modern life, or for nervous babies, which might be the same thing. The harried book people under the unnatural lights do not look at ease; they look tired.

I'm not here for my good looks either. My publishers have me shaking hands with the world. At night, we do what we do so well. We party. The moon is full, the velvety air of romantic old New Orleans caresses the exposed arms and legs of the swaying couples under the banana trees. The siren song of Café Brazil throws erotic shivers through the throng. Reading is the farthest thing from our minds.

The Less We Know

The less we know about anything, the more information we have on it; and the more information we have, the less we know. Take cookbooks, for instance. In the old days when people really cooked, all a family needed was a greasy card file full of everyday recipes and one well-thumbed cookbook for holidays and special occasions. Life in the kitchen back then was routine, interrupted now and then by a weird experiment: when the noodles turned green everyone knew that Mom was upset. These days, however, nobody cooks but everybody has cookbooks—dozens of them. They take the place in the kitchen formerly reserved for basics like flour and sugar. We read them while we wait for the microwave to do its job. Dreaming of exotic food, we gobble irradiated slop. In the bookstore, the place formerly reserved for books to be read has also been taken over by cookbooks, which bear the same relation to real books that microwave food bears to your grandmother's.

In every sphere, experience and know-how have been replaced by how-to books, and these same pseudo-books have in turn usurped literature. Meeting and talking to people has been replaced by books on how to meet and talk to them, and these too have replaced real books, the ones you can *read*. Books that help one maintain a desired lifestyle have replaced books that can really help you with *life*. And what happens to the life such books replace? The same thing that happens to the books these books displace. It and they disappear, and the lifestyle specialists take over. Cooking becomes the province of professional cooks. Even one's social life becomes managed by professionals—if one can afford it.

And therein lies the saving grace: reality disappears only for those who can afford it. The poor don't buy cookbooks: *The Silver Palate* can't be got with food stamps. The poor just go on consulting their handed-down card file and well-thumbed *Joy of Cooking*. They can't pay to have their lives managed, either; they just have to get on with them. Now if only they could escape the mess poverty makes out of them, they could save us all.

The Star System

"The heavens," said Frank O'Hara, "move on the star system." He was writing an ode to the cinema, and stars are big indeed in that firmament. How big can be occasionally glimpsed by mortals when they open their morning paper and there find that Dustin Hoffman has signed a deal for $6,300,000 plus 22.5 percent of his next movie. That could amount to the same as Sylvester "Rambo" Stallone's fat $12,000,000, or more, depending on how starry-eyed *we* get. It doesn't take a math genius to figure out that after Dustin and Rambo take their cut, there isn't a hell of a lot left for anyone else. The figures themselves are only vaguely comprehensible: they equal the entire yearly budgets of certain countries. Should Dustin or Sylvester wish to arm a guerrilla force and overthrow a government somewhere, they could easily do it on the advance from their next picture. Most of us are used to thinking of money in terms of its use. But what can one possibly use that much money for? Besides being a ripoff of everyone around it, that kind of money murders the imagination.

Things haven't been much better lately in the nearer galaxies, publishing for instance. Publishers have been giving huge advances to one or two stars while starving everyone else. In a noble if somewhat vague gesture, Stephen King, the best-selling nightmare factory, took a $1 advance for *Christine*, which became a hard-cover and paperback best-seller. Recently, Gregory MacDonald, another popular author, took a symbolic $10 advance on his new book. Those are fine gestures but, remember, we are talking *advances against royalties*. Once those royalties start rolling in, you can bet your favorite pair of blue jeans that neither King nor MacDonald will be giving back a cent. And why should they? It's in the nature of things to grow, even to obscene proportions. We made them stars, so let them roll above us, roll us, and fatten their rolls.

Britannica a Hoax?

A disgruntled employee who tried to sabotage the *Encyclopaedia Britannica* by secretly rewriting history was thwarted by the publishers' sophisticated computer. It appears that the disgruntled employee had been substituting the name of Allah for that of Jesus Christ in certain passages.

I wonder what happened before such sophisticated computers were in existence. It is possible that in the long, dark years before the computer, also known as B.C., disgruntled employees were also rewriting history. Perhaps history as we know it, thanks in large part to the *Britannica*, is entirely the work of disgruntled employees. It is even possible that a disgruntled employee in, let's say, 1934 B.C. secretly substituted the name of Jesus Christ for that of Allah. Entire armies of students went forth into the world to act on the basis of that view of history. When Britain was an empire its soldiers, when not busy making history, were certainly reading it. The reading of it no doubt colored their making of it so that the final product, the British Empire, could very well have been the fruit of disgruntled employees.

Tampering with history in B.C. was not limited to the *Britannica*. Books everywhere go into their final stages through the hands of obscure and possibly disgruntled employees. Copy editors, typesetters, proofreaders, and printers are all potentially dangerous rewriters of history. If enough of them have tampered with enough history, I would not be surprised if everything we know is not, in fact, erroneous. Which would explain why things just aren't right in history. And why one person's history differs wildly from another's. And why in certain places the deity is named Allah and in others, Jesus Christ. And why there is doubt as to dates, and why there are different calendars. Even languages may be, in the final analysis, the result of sabotage and disaffection. There was only one language before Babel and then the disgruntled employees began tampering with it while speaking it. With the advent of writing, tampering became generalized.

Language and history are a colossal act of sabotage. But in the current era, A.C.—After Computers—all that is changed.

In from the Rain

The clouds burst open violently and all of us on the street took shelter quickly. Some dashed into a shoe store where a nine-dollar sale has been in progress for a year, but I dashed into the bookstore next to it, and so did about fifty others. I love being in a bookstore in the rain. Big, splashing deluge outside—who knows? maybe the Flood, the End of the World—and here I am, cozy, surrounded by all I could ever want to read.

I scanned my riches and was about to bury myself in late-breaking literature when I noticed my fellow refugees. Most of them had backed into the bookcases flanking the entrance and had frozen there. They stood stiffly, looking out at the rain, turning their heads neither right nor left nor behind them. It was as if the books . . . embarrassed them. They were trying to avoid contact with them. Go ahead, I silently urged them, they won't bite you. But they stood there, staring fixedly at the rain outside, brought to a halt before those front bookcases like flu germs before the blood-brain barrier.

Some were sniffling with fear, or perhaps even hostility. And then it struck me: THESE PEOPLE HATE BOOKS! AND THEY FEEL GUILTY ABOUT IT! I saw that only two of the fifty or so had ventured so far from the door as the magazine rack. And I saw that the reader, that mythical creature for whom books come into being, was no more. Not only are there no more readers, there aren't even book thieves any more. Not even those sideways glances denoting petty theft pertained in this crowd. Of course, if this *is* the Final Deluge, I gleefully thought, they will have to get over it. They will have to stay here and read everything, even decide which books to eat in order to survive and which books to keep in order to live, and fights will break out over what books to eat and what books to read. And then the rain stopped and there was a sudden stampede for the door, where the crowd merged briefly with the crowd next door which was carrying unmistakable bundles of nine-dollar shoes either in bags or under their coats.

Literary Touring

I saw the house in Saint Louis where William Burroughs was born, and I took a leaf from the yard. Not far from it is the building where Tennessee Williams wrote *The Glass Menagerie*. It's now called The Glass Menagerie Apartments, with apartments going, I guessed, for about $250 per month for an efficiency. I took an autumn leaf from this yard too, and a berry from some kind of bush. Two streets over was where T. S. Eliot had been born, but the house was gone and now a freeway went through. The massive shadow of the Saint Louis Cathedral fell over the place where the house had stood, as it must have done in the days when little T. S. ambled about in shorts. The freeway and the church shadow were perfect Eliot, standing as they did for the future, which he despised, and the past, which he lamented.

Saint Louis doesn't hold its literary sites in very high regard. The places I just mentioned I discovered with the aid of a painful little homemade pamphlet full of errors and whimsy. Burroughs's house wasn't even in it—I got the address from a bookstore clerk. Other American cities aren't much better. Baltimore made Edgar Allan Poe's house a museum only a few years back, when the city fathers decided he'd be good tourist biz. The Whitman house in Camden, New Jersey, stands all by itself in a former slum, managed beautifully if modestly by someone who has to work a second job nearby. In New Orleans it took me hours to locate Audubon's house in the French Quarter. There is no marker.

In contrast to all this, the French worship their writers. They like them better than politicians and generals. There are signs of their passing everywhere, on buildings and in streets. People go to the Père-Lachaise cemetery to have picnics with Balzac and Proust. I go there every winter to visit Guillaume Apollinaire and Jim Morrison.

Our urban planners and developers should have to pass a literary history test—administered by the French.

Bukowski on the Bus

The man across the aisle from me took off his legs and I was trying not to look at the stumps. I did anyway. They were pointy cones of flesh ending just below the knees. I concentrated on my reading and succeeded in banishing the image. A little later, I couldn't help overhearing him. He was telling the guy just behind me about the difficulty of negotiating the aisle to the bathroom without legs on a moving bus. "No guidance system," he said, and I gathered from that that he was a vet, probably had his legs blown off in Vietnam. He had a pleasant face with a beard and long gray hair. I followed his conversation along with the new poems of Charles Bukowski that I was reading. His comments and Bukowski's poetry dovetailed perfectly. A spoken witticism would be followed by a written quip. The talker began to match the poet profanity for profanity. They were riffing in tandem.

The legless man was going all the way to Florida on this bus, a twelve-hour trip. I was getting off in New Orleans in ten minutes. I turned around and gave him the book. "Something to read on the way," I said. He picked up the tome, a big nice new twenty-dollar hardback, opened it once and said, "Oh, it's poetry! I can't read that stuff!" "This is different," I said, "he tells little stories. Read one." He did. Then he handed it back. "Still poetry," he said.

The guy sitting just behind him, a heavily tattooed gent in a sleeveless Levi's jacket, said, "Lemme see that!" I handed him the book, whereupon he started to read it. Five minutes later he was still reading. Only three minutes to New Orleans now, and I was sure I'd made a score. I was determined to give Bukowski away on this bus no matter what. This was his natural constituency. Only a few years ago, poetry was like drugs to people on buses and trains. "Poetry? Oh, wow! Far out! Got more?"

The bus pulled into the station. I stood up. Got my bag. Felt a tap on my shoulder. It was the tattooed guy handing me back the book. "Neah," he said.

Trailer

There was a trailer parked on campus with one of the four copies of the Magna Carta inside. There were long lines of people waiting to see it, the first manifesto of civil liberties, the document on which the Constitution is based. The trailer was spacious enough inside to contain exhibits along the walls, forty people, and a very fat policeman who stood behind the glass case containing the distinguished parchment from England. The text was in faded Latin but there was no mistaking the reverence with which we all gazed upon it. But I was equally amazed by the trailer.

"We could really live in one of these," I whispered to my mate, confessing a dream I've secretly had for several years. I saw my first trailer in a trailer camp in California. It seemed to me then, and still does, that the camp was the ideal community, the trailer the perfect habitat toward which all human society has been striving ever since we began making polities. The tension between moving and staying put was at last gracefully solved. We have all seen the city, the suburb, the small town, and the village change under the impact of the car. The city became a suburb, the small town a rest stop on the highway. People got lost and communities weakened. Only the trailer allows you to take both your habitat and your community with you while you move at the same time.

I have wondered for some time why trailer parks don't have their own literature the way the city, the suburb, and the small town do. Maybe it's because writers—with the exception of poets—have been sedentary creatures dependent on a fixed address for their mail. That isn't a good reason any longer—not with computers and modems on the scene. "Maybe I'll be the Homer of trailer camps," I whispered to my mate as she tried hard to decipher the Latin of the text on which our democracy is based. "It's the trailer," I said, "that's the last word in constitutional liberty!" The Magna Carta was the beginning and the trailer is the end—and we were all in it, parked for a moment.

The Greyhound Monopoly

Greyhound swallowed Trailways and now monopolizes bus transport in the U.S.A. It happened quietly one night—and neither peep nor squeak was heard from anyone. Who was going to squawk? Not the woman with five children running away from her abusive husband to a new life on the other coast. Not the soldier going home on leave in his uniform with a suitcase tied up with string. Not the idiot savant recently freed from an asylum spouting fiery words from a burning brain. Not the consumptive country boy helped on by a federal marshall at a country crossroads. Not the four Chicanos going to find work in the sugarcane fields for five dollars a day. No, Greyhound is now a monopoly, and there is nobody out there to blow the whistle on deteriorating service, increasing rudeness, escalating fares, disappearing routes. Greyhound is now *the* interstate carrier of the dispossessed, the voiceless, the Americans one never sees on TV.

And yet, how much better off are middle-class Americans, isolated like laboratory cultures in the single cells of their cars? Cut off from their fellow beings, going to work in sanitized cubicles, isolated by television and condoms from body contact, they have been exiled into a distance far lonelier than that of the bus riders. Inside the smoke-filled Greyhound groaning under the weight of coughing children, hapless adults, and their misshapen belongings, a certain camaraderie reigns. This may well be the last human community in America. It flowers briefly in spontaneous exchange, based on the profound understanding that poverty returns one's humanity to one.

The lonely beings in cars and bars and offices pay more and more to meet in the partitioned sanction of monitored tourist zones. No sweet poverty and anarchy can touch them and return them to a sense of the human adventure. The suburban mind has eaten the streets with its morning croissant, and there is no place now for the folks on the Greyhound to get off. In fact, why *should* they get off? a sensible planner will one day ask. Put the poor on buses and keep them moving, always moving. That way, they won't be anywhere long enough to vote or to talk about it. They will become a memory, a forgotten dream of a time when powerless people found joy in their shared strangeness.

Surreal Jobs

There are some strange jobs in this world. My friend Larry once had a job nailing Jesus to the cross. Literally. The crosses came from Bolivia, and the Jesuses came from Brazil. The place he worked for, in Tulsa, Oklahoma, put them together and sold them in religious shops. He didn't feel too good about it. But a job's a job.

The weirdest job I ever had was stamping little pieces of leather with a machine stamp as they went by on a conveyor belt. This was in a sweatshop in midtown Manhattan and no one, including myself, spoke English there. The machine made an infernal noise. I went out for lunch one day and never came back. Didn't even bother to collect my measly pay.

Alice used to work at the lost-and-found at Wayne State University in Detroit. That's where I met her. Every day people brought in umbrellas. She sat there surrounded by thousands of umbrellas like a strange rain goddess. Nobody ever claimed them so she made presents of them to strangers who looked depressed. "You look rained on," she'd say, and hand them an umbrella. Once somebody brought in a lost ten-dollar bill. We got ten bags of White Castle hamburgers for the lost souls on Cass Avenue.

My friend David once went to ten different psychiatrists and tape-recorded his conversations with them. He was pretending to be crazy for an article some magazine editor had paid him to write. The psychiatrists were each of a different persuasion, from the Freudian to the Rogerian. David never wrote the article—he went crazy instead.

Another writer I knew was nearly killed by research. He tried to live on mail-order food for six months to see if it could be done. He ate stuff from boxes and cans until he turned a very odd color. If you have to, he concluded, go for Chinese mail-food. Stay away from Mexican. The tamales disintegrate even if they hand-cancel them at the post office.

Hand-canceling tamales: another weird job, come to think of it.

The Return of the Amateur

A medical textbook salesman told me that the new medical textbooks are like comic books compared to the old ones. They are simplistically written and offer little understanding of the body as a whole. "Don't count on the coming doctors," he said. "They'll know nothing without machines." After this aside, he went on to talk about the football strike. But he hadn't really changed subjects. The delight the fans are taking in scab football, he said, is a perfect picture of this "second best" world we live in. People like second-string football players because they fumble, fall, and injure themselves. The perfection of pro players has been boring everyone for years.

This fact has not escaped the media watchers, the salesman declared. They know that the amateur games have "higher entertainment value" than the official ones. They know that perfection is less entertaining than awkwardness, that professionalism is, in fact, not amusing at all. "Nothing wrong with amateurs," he added. "Don't get me wrong. I'm an amateur myself. I have the desire but I'm insufficiently prepared, just like most people. But I'm not sure if I'd like the 'B' students of the world to run things more than they already do—you know, secretaries who can't type, doctors who are lost without machines, politicians who can't make a speech, writers who can't write, editors who don't edit, builders who erect approximations, watchmen who fall asleep on the job. The President, after all, is first and foremost an actor." Here the salesman paused. "I did vote for him, though," he added, sounding perplexed.

I read, in that perplexed pause, a common dilemma. We want our professionals to pretend that they are amateurs so that they can amuse us. But we don't *really* want our presidents and doctors to be amateurs. Still, we suspect professionalism and do not want to admit that anyone knows more than we do, because deep down we feel that we know everything and that what we don't know is somehow *evil*. We equate amateurishness with innocence. After all, wasn't knowledge the original sin? In paradise, before history began, there lived two perfect amateurs. After eating from the tree they acquired the know-how of pleasure. It was the first step toward professionalism. Adam and Eve made themselves *separate*. For this they were condemned to live in time, in history. History is the story of increasing specialization, of always leaving behind some state of innocence for an increased knowledge that always increases our unhappiness. Staying an amateur is perhaps our only defense against losing more of our innocence than we already have.

But history, and our own species, proves that we can never really go back to the garden. And so, in this postmodern age of ours, we do what we have learned to do best: we *pretend*. We pretend to be amateurs, we pretend to be like everyone else, we go to great lengths to reassure everyone that we are just like everyone else. We reserve our professionalism for the depths of the laboratory, the solitude of the writing chamber, the interior of the data bank. When we emerge it is as if from a dirty deed, a sin. When we leave the inner sanctum where we commit our professional deeds, we act as if they never occurred. We cheer with the mass, try hard to integrate ourselves into the great democratic body whose activity as a whole is to pretend innocence, naiveté, amazement at the spectacles of the media. But it's a fraudulent effort: we all know more than we let on; we work hard to appear simple.

I thought of my friend A., a painter, who could paint incredibly well but could sell nothing. After years of unsuccessful hustle, he started painting badly, something that wasn't easy for him at all. Now he sells. It isn't a matter of right or wrong, he tells me, it's a matter of timeliness. This is the time of 'B' students, so let's play ball! But in effect, what A. has done is to transform himself into a professional of badness, a master of the awkward stroke that is the going thing.

I turned to the medical textbook salesman to tell him the story of my friend the painter, but he had already started talking golf with the Cliffs Notes salesman on his right.

Lunch on Continental

I don't know why you would want to, but if you would like to reduce a peasant to tears, serve him lunch on Continental Airlines. The package consists of several packages of varying sizes that open cleverly into one another. It's a snug fit between the two kinds of cheese, the crackers, the cake, and the condiments. After they are budged they will not go back together again: something profound, like the loss of virginity, has occurred in the structural makeup of the package. But, all right, who needs to put lunch back together anyway? You might as well eat it.

One piece of cheese is a triangular chunk of chalk-white pseudo-Swiss cream cheese wrapped up in a filmy clear plastic. To open it you tug at the end of a red plastic thread which is supposed to dangle free but is invariably trapped under the wrapper. If you succeed in nabbing this thread end, either with your very sharp pinkie nail or your fang if you're a vampire, you must guard against its breaking, which it will undoubtedly do about midway through its journey around the cheese. To control the resultant rage, gently set aside this *faux fromage* and turn your attention to the other piece.

This cheese is sliced yellow American cheese and its cover is tougher, consisting as it does of hard, though more honest, American plastic. This rugged, airtight cover can be removed only by stabs with a sharp knife, which the airline does not provide. Instead it gives you a rounded plastic paddle, which is tightly wrapped in yet another variety of plastic at the bottom of the styrofoam tray that supports *all* the little packages like the foundation of Saint Peter's.

Should you find yourself unable to release the yellow cheese too, go on to the crackers. Though wrapped well in waxed paper, they are not intractable. They will, however, crumble should you apply the slightest excess of pressure—and you always do. If you haven't beaten this whole lunch to a pulp with your fists, you might now consider the cake. It is unwrapped, but as it is made wholly of sheer unadulterated plastic, your bowels may have trouble unwrapping it later.

I sat weeping before this lunch the other day, hoping against hope that Continental would hurry up and get me to where I was going before I lost my mind. I could not imagine what a less technologically savvy being would do with this package. I mean, I could, but it is too horrifying to contemplate.

That "At Home" Feeling

We have good, wide beds, the ad said. We wear soft shoes made out of squeak-proof rubber as we tiptoe reassuringly about. The lights are dim and the music nearly inaudible, though always pleasant. And the food, *ah*! The food is superb, the latest in nutrition, and delicious, too. "They treated me like someone special," a voice said. "I felt that I was more than a number." And then there were pictures of big, pastel-colored machines tended lovingly by good-natured humans bent tenderly over them. You can lie back, smile, meditate, enjoy. It's wonderful, the ad said. Come to us. We're General Hospital. We offer you the latest in maternity packages. Cutting-edge oncology. Splendid chemotherapy. Lovely gastrointestinal probes. Mellifluous scans. Exquisite colostomies.

I think I'll check right in. Sounds better than Club Med, if you ask me. All those machines and meals and music and not a care in the world! I know I'm not sick, but so what? I'll get sick *sometime*, and I want to be *there* when I do.

As hospitals compete more and more, things should get even comfier. There will be dances and theater and entertainment of all sorts. Performers on their last legs will entertain patients on theirs. There will be bets on who will and won't last the evening. The hospitals will offer package deals: half off to anyone who can bring in another sick person! Sick people will cultivate sick friends or, failing that, will make healthy friends sick and drag them to their favorite hospital. The hospitals themselves will be great architectural wonders booked solid for years in advance.

Yes, the future looks healthy for the ill.

Everybody's in Jail

One of every thirty-five men in the United States is in prison, on probation, or under parole supervision, according to a Bureau of Justice statistic. That's a staggering figure. Every thirty-fifth man is a convicted lawbreaker. What is it? Do we have a criminal gene, or do we live in a forest of laws so thick that the only way we can see clear is to break a few of them? Or is the criminal, as Karl Marx thought, too productive a force for society to do without? After all, the criminal produces cops, lawyers, detectives, judges, jailers, locksmiths, probation officers, courtroom reporters and even art, literature, drama, and morality. Furthermore, Marx points out, the development of science is largely a response to the criminal, who not only provides the need for such fields as forensic medicine and security technology but stimulates productive forces by jolting the spirit from boredom and stagnation.

That's one way to account for the energy of crime, the equally energetic pursuit of it, and even its relentless glorification in popular culture. But it can be equally argued that with so many minds and hands behind bars, society suffers a diminishing of energy. It's bad enough that the military buildup steals most of our energy to invest it in an imaginary common defense. Do we also need to invest what's left of this energy for personal defense? If most of us spend time and money keeping the rest of us locked up, there is, it seems to me, precious little left over for any real productivity. What we need is a new definition of crime which includes those things that injure us collectively, not just individually. Instead of legislating morality, like drug use, we should be punishing polluting industries, unfair taxation to finance doomsday weapons, and all other attempts at energy theft. I bet the economic indicators, as well as the Bureau of Justice statistics, would change dramatically if we recognized that we are all in this together.

Dummies

E scape is the art of our time. A few years ago, two Romani-
ans escaped from their native country in a crawl space
made by placing a fake ceiling over the real ceiling of a Vienna-
bound train. They emerged five days later, and were photo-
graphed proudly holding their fake ceiling for press photogra-
phers.

The latest artistic escape was the creation of Heinz Braun,
who escaped from East Germany by driving a car with three
high-ranking Soviet officers in it. The Soviets sat stiffly through
the border crossing, their haughty manner familiar to the
guards. Only they were neither Soviets nor officers but dum-
mies, skillfully sculpted by Herr Braun.

This is a most hopeful development, for people as well as for
art. Individuals have always used dummies to slip through the
inattention of officials. Lately, inattention is becoming the
prevailing mode of supervision in the Soviet world. A story is
told of a border guard in Bulgaria who came to work one day,
saw himself sitting in his usual tower, and went back home to
sleep. The eyes of supervisors are glazed over with boredom. If
the trend continues, whole cities may be able to escape by
arranging dummies to take the places of people at work, in
restaurants, in parks.

Not that things are much different in the West, dummy-wise
Here we try to escape artfully from other problems. In the Bron
a few years back, the city tried to outwit would-be squatters by
putting decals of people in the windows of abandoned build-
ings. Housewives ironing, guys drinking beer, stuff like that.
Only tourists would have been fooled, and there haven't been
any in the Bronx since the last presidential candidates. The

Bronx couldn't escape the squatters any more than those border guards could escape from themselves.

Once in a while, a daring artist makes it over the wall. Once in a while, a prisoner makes a good replica of himself on a cell cot. If artists used to live in ivory towers to escape from life, they are now finally learning to escape from towers to get back to life.

But these are still singular efforts. No one knows yet how to make an escape art good enough for whole neighborhoods, whole countries, whole peoples.

How a Body Meets a Thing

We are moving. Again. And as always, we stand astonished before the numbers of things we have drawn about our persons. Wherefrom these knickknacks? Wherefrom these dishes, spoons, and forks? Wherefrom these folders? These cabinets? These plants? These shirts? These shoes? Like a relentless tide, they wash over our bodies and stay, these things, these *objets*, these fillers of closets, rooms, and lives.

I like to look straight out, my vision unimpeded. But the horizon is crowded with mountains of stuff, the imperative junk of consumer goods. Even my peripheral vision is taken with store-bought things. If I die and there is a hell, my hell will be a shopping mall. I will trudge down its aisles forever, with only rides on the escalators for relief.

When we came here, I tell everyone, we came with only a suitcase. Now look! It was Pandora's suitcase. That suitcase had, in fact, been the artful result of a steady divestiture of things from our old house. We had open-till-dawn yard sales, giveaways, and throwaways until we got it all down to one suitcase containing the essentials: things we made with our hands— poems and pictures. Sure enough, as soon as we moved into the new house, things clustered about the suitcase, burying it and us under their passive weight. And now, once again, we have resurrected the suitcase, and are beginning the major work of divestiture. But it is harder. Every move we make, it is harder and harder to tell where we end and where things begin. A certain chair will slowly but firmly attach itself to one's behind. A flowerpot will hover perpetually under the watering can attached to an outstretched arm. Bit by bit one begins to lose the human outline and make a sort of symbiotic lump with the things around. Most beings in our time are hidden like faint pulses inside large contraptions of things glued together. They move clumsily to and fro inside these junk heaps, wondering what happened to their suitcase and their youth.

Anybody want to buy a couch?

On the Road

I 've been on the road. Palm Beach; San Francisco; Berkeley; Ashland, Oregon; Normal, Illinois; Cleveland; Akron; Kent, Ohio. At the risk of sounding like a born-again nouveau American, I'll say it loud: This country's wonderfully different wherever you go! I used to think that just because there are McDonald'ses everywhere, there is no point in leaving home. Well, I was wrong.

Palm Beach has a golden pink light capable of holding both the old and the poor and the rich and the spoiled. San Francisco is still foggy in one part while sunny in another. Its $1,000-a-month studio apartments rented to young Japanese businessmen stand above the crowded dwellings of Chinatown where Hong Kong émigrés room with their relations. Telegraph Avenue in Berkeley holds on to a countercultural shabbiness even as Durant experiences yuppie vertigo. Ashland, Oregon, with its Shakespeare theater, is home to the ecologically sensitive who think California is a garbage dump. (You can't build a house in Oregon if it throws a shadow on the side of the neighbor's house where the solar panel should go.) In Normal, Illinois, in the middle of flat Spring country, students worry about being isolated and out of touch with the world. In Cleveland, there is a feeling that the Rock 'n' Roll Hall of Fame and the success of the Indians will bring the city back from the pits of depression. In Akron, at the World of Rubber Museum, the curio seekers buy out the blimps and the tire ashtrays. In Kent, they continue to remember the four students killed twenty years ago by the Ohio National Guard. A memorial will finally be built.

And the people in these places! Wonderful, alive to a sense of place! I am delighted and humbled to find everywhere like this. In Oregon, the mountains are covered with snow. In Cleveland, a flame jets out of a steel chimney into the night sky.

The airplane insists on erasing distance. The places and people I've encountered insist it still exists.

I make myself transparent to take it all in.

Arches

Saint Louis, city of narrow escapes! There is an arch there in Saint Louis, by the Mississippi River. Called variously the Jefferson National Expansion Memorial, the Gateway to the West, or simply the Arch, it is a statement of imperial sculptural power. Its 630 feet of stainless steel soar into the winter sky: there is no talking back to it.

It scared me witless. There is a little elevator in it that goes to the top, up one side for ten minutes, down the other for ten more. I wanted to go up, if only to overcome my fear of imperial monuments. Michael Castro, a poet who was showing me around, tried to caution against it. He'd taken some of his relatives up. Had no desire to go back. But I insisted. I have been scared of such monuments ever since I can remember. I haven't yet been able to go under the Arc de Triomphe in Paris or the Arch of Titus in Rome. When I look at them I hear the sound of marching boots and something old in me bids me to flee. Gypsies don't like empires. I am a part of the nomad world that has skirted around the borders of empires since time began. Of course, there are few nomads left and the empires have grown so huge they now contain everything inside their borders. Nomads have become secretive and furtive. At our peak we rode with Genghis Khan, at our nadir we move through the global village careful of arches and other symbols of power.

As we waited our turn to go up in the Arch, I gripped the railing tightly and strained to overcome my historical vertigo. I told myself that the Saint Louis Arch, for all its impressive force, is only half the arch of McDonald's, a friendlier symbol, no? But when the door opened to the windowless capsule that took one to the top, I turned around and split. Call it blind panic, but it felt great! Michael, running after me, understood perfectly. Poets are all nomads: being sealed in steel capsules inside the symbols of power does not appeal to them.

Texas

Texas lives its clichés. It's big, it's rude, it's stormy. There are real men there. They wear their boots to sleep in the back of their pickups. They get their 72-ounce steak free if they can eat it in one hour. They dance to real cowboy songs like "The Orange Blossom Special," and they drive like maniacs. The road signs say BRAG ABOUT TEXAS, and then, as an afterthought, DRIVE FRIENDLY. Around Houston the roads are swarming with a species of Texan fed on steak and oil who looks descended from TV soaps. Actually, the oil's been feeding fewer and fewer Texans lately, and that 72- ounce steak is now more likely to be beans and rice—that is, when it isn't chicken spaghetti, seafood frog legs, seashell shrimp or, of course, that ubiquitous American road staple, Gas Food, or the full dinner, Gas Food Lodging.

I measure distance by dead armadillos, which form a natural and regular break in the immensity of the southern desert. I write in my journal, likewise breaking paragraphs with little drawings of dead armadillos. An indigenous Texas poetry will shortly arise, I'm certain, with dead armadillo stanza breaks.

Little country churches spring from the mesquite and the sage: Aboundant Life, Inc.; Fellowship of Excitement; Yucca and the Holy Family. This is the kind of place where saints come from and faces appear in the tortillas. This is also where Mary manifests herself before little girls herding longhorns through the oil wells. And at NASA near Houston, I see another religious vignette: ten guys with guns stand by while two repairmen fix a broken traffic light. This work cult may not be unique to Texas, however. Throughout the South one can see groups of workmen standing around a solitary worker, particularly on weekends and after working hours. This is called the Worship of Overtime in the Church of the *Dolce Far Niente*.

Pancakes and coffee west of the Pecos at sunset put the whole state neatly into the postcard prepared for it beforehand. There is another postcard behind this one, and another. And somewhere, deep in the heart of it, the postcards stop and the movies begin, things like *Paris, Texas*, and *The Seekers* with John Wayne, the once and always Duke.

In a car one is always at the movies, and in Texas one is always in a car.

Kansas

K ansas is the West, not the Midwest. I try to correct this general misapprehension because it was mine, too, before I got there. In Lawrence they've stuffed a horse from Custer's last stand. It's a little water-damaged now but it stands its ground stiffly. The people walk Western, their toes pointing out. The whiskey is strong. At one party I went to, the host apologized because the police hadn't yet busted up the festivities. "I don't know," he said wistfully. "They busted every other party we had!" Of rugged Kansas individualism they tell many stories. It seems that at the turn of the century, Standard Oil tried to give Kansas a raw deal. The university in Lawrence gave up its athletic field so that the state could build its own refinery there. Take *that*, Standard! If LSU had done that, Louisiana would have been a different place. It would be Western.

The day I came to Kansas, Alf Landon had just turned a hundred. The President mugged for pictures with the old senator in his porch rocker. But Ronald Reagan wasn't the only President then visiting the state. Allen Ginsberg, the President of Poetry, was also there to celebrate the twenty-year reunion of various free spirits who had lived there in the 1960s. Some of them, like William Burroughs, still live nearby, after wide detours through Morocco and New York. Present also were Ed Sanders, who went to school there, Robert Creeley, who is much beloved there, and Timothy Leary, who was there in spirit only when everyone was "turning on, tuning in, and dropping out"— and many others, including me, *Time* magazine, *Der Stern*, and the stuffed horse. Allen Ginsberg sang, Timothy Leary did stand-up comedy, William Burroughs delivered the news from hell, dozens of children in torn jeans jumped fully clothed into a swimming pool, and the prairie grasses made everyone weep. Someone asked me what happened to the radical Left, and I looked behind me and then to every side but all there was was prairie as far as the eye could see.

We were in Kansas.

Carlsbad

I have descended into the underworld at Carlsbad Cavern in New Mexico and communed with the emperor of bats. Two hundred and fifty thousand of his minions take off at dusk from Carlsbad and consume every insect their side of the Pecos. The cavern itself is like visiting one's brain in a dream. Minerals grow in the vast dark interior with a kind of resolute beauty that negates time. The deeper one goes the more peaceful one feels. It is here, of course, that the human journey began, among the mirror pools, the limestone pillars, the stone lace, the mountains of guano. We are in the womb here; it is eternally 66 degrees, forever and ever the primal scene.

Carlsbad is the exact realization of the fantastic as it appeared to me in childhood when I gazed in wonder at the illustrations in Jules Verne. Doré didn't invent. No one invents anything. Here are the ghost ships, the altars, the gods, the royal chambers, the magic mirrors. I have been noticing, in fact, how much of the magic in old European fantasies is actually in America. I have found the magic worlds depicted in old nineteenth-century woodcuts, for instance, in the Louisiana swamps with their eerie moss in the morning fog. The fantastic, as the Europeans imagined it, was the New World. Its newness has long since vanished in most, but not all, places. Here at Carlsbad it continues, its fantastic aspect not diminished by reality. Near the bottom of the cavern I begin to think that humans may have made a mistake in emerging from the caves to conquer the planet's surface. We should have stayed here among the internal landscapes of the earth's womb to evolve into a whole different kind of creature, a blind and magical being.

After three hours of negotiating the steep walks of the cave, one comes at last to a brightly lit vision: nestled under the great stone vaults are round counters where film, postcards, and hot dogs are being sold. Circular neon buzzes above the concessions as tourists swarm around them, grateful for the return to the present. We eat candy bars and buy film, and I imagine for a moment that we are the survivors of the Third World War living here on hot dogs while waiting for the radiation to clear.

The world may yet end as it began.

Paradise

I have been suspicious of paradises ever since I was expelled from the womb, and have quite precise arguments against them. For one thing, the weather in Paradise, by being always perfect, never corresponds to your psychic weather. If it doesn't rain when you're depressed you'll feel twice as bad. And for another, there is no strife in Paradise and I believe in strife. Strife, which includes miserable weather and ugly buildings, is what spurs me to action. If there is nothing to fight, what's the point in getting up in the morning?

When I arrived in Hawaii I was fully prepared to resist heavenly enticements, including, most specifically, the subversive aroma of huge flowers which have been known in all cultures to still the urge to combat. But it wasn't the flowers on the hills that altered me, though they were huge, aromatic, and bright. Nor was it the vast sky jammed with stars and the full moon under which the powerful waves of the Pacific made strong music. And even the allure of tropical fish, among which I put my masked face allowing them to kiss the glass around my eyes, had only tangential effect. What got me, finally, after I arrived on the Big Island and was taken to the little village of Volcano on the edge of a huge but by no means dead crater, was the Goddess Pele.

The Goddess Pele is alive in the body of this new earth which continues being created even as we speak. New lava flows are adding to it as much as we lose to coastal erosion in Louisiana every year. The newness of creation clings to everything. Wild orchids, coconut trees, passion fruit, guava, and bananas grow from the barely cooled lava of this restless Paradise.

The natives have seen the Goddess. My friend Faye saw her, a woman in red, when she was camping near Mauna Loa, which is spewing hot lava into the ocean again. Others have seen her in fires and in volcanic steam, on black sand beaches and in waterfalls. In the Volcano Arts Center there is a glass case full of letters from people returning rocks to Pele. "I came home and broke my leg—my wife left me—I lost my job—please return these two rocks to Goddess Pele and ask her forgiveness." Pele is, like all gods, jealous of what she makes. I made sure to take nothing back with me but flowers.

My friends took me bathing in volcanic steam at the edge of the crater. Five feet from us was the immense hole into which I wouldn't have minded diving if I had been so inclined. I had always thought that jumping from buildings and bridges is silly, but leaping into the fiery core of the earth appeals to me. As I crouched there in the heat of the rock, I knew whence I'd come and what my planet and body were made of. I knew also that the Hawaiian islands had had a tragic history and that, like other paradises, they had been victimized by our greed for spices. There are racial tensions in Paradise, and the pressure of development. Talking to Hawaiians I felt profoundly my humble station as a tourist. They spoke of pollution (including tourism), greed, and Japanese investments. I was shown a vast lava mass on the side of a mountain where you could still see parts of house roofs and cars sticking out. An unwise developer put buildings there without asking the goddess. Now look.

Sweating in the nocturnal volcanic steam, so close to the primal fire, I somehow knew that the Pacific goddess could take care of herself. Of course, she needed help. I realized that Paradise, at least on earth, needs all the help it can get. After all, most places that we have now given up on, like Love Canal, New York, or Baton Rouge, Louisiana, were once paradises. Pele had certainly and swiftly gained my allegiance. Far from lacking in strife, her domain was the very stuff of it. The fact that Paradise still exists, even if sorely threatened, felt like an inducement to fight when I returned to hell.

Fish Out Your Window

There is a hotel in Seattle, The Edgewater, where they let you fish out your window. In fact, they encourage you. They say FISH OUT YOUR WINDOW! right in front. The evening I checked in, a horrifying scene was unfolding in the room immediately below mine: a puffing couple was wrestling with a small shark. They at last let it go, and off it went, hook in cheek into the cold water of Puget Sound.

The following morning there was an earthquake and the bed shook. Yes, I was in a place where nature seemed to mimic my dreams. (I've been having ferocious dreams lately. I barely lie down to sleep when an immense carnage is unleashed. People are dragged off behind horses, and red-eyed monsters beat each other to a pulp.) Later that day a man on the street gave me a pamphlet when he overheard that I was from Louisiana. It's called "Animal Agony in Addiction Research," and it contains horrible pictures of animals fried on megadoses of drugs. The man said that in Louisiana they do some of the worst things. That would explain some of the dreams I have there: the agony of the animals floats at night into the minds of queasy folk like myself.

My violent nights are not the only ones in my house. My younger son has been standing bolt upright in his bed in the dark hours, screaming about being kidnapped. I know where that comes from: the mass hysteria about kidnapped children that pervades the air of America right down to the carton you pour milk on your morning cereal from. The public airwaves put forth a steady dose of paranoia. It's a constant hum composed of environmental dangers, tortured animals, and kidnapped children. The only thing is, the first two are real, the last one is just the business of fear. But dreams make no distinctions; they feed on images, not facts.

In the daytime the hum is bearable. At night, the sharks swim right up to the window, and you go fishing.

Is Normal Normal?

I went to Normal, Illinois. My friend David and I took each other's picture under the sign that says WELCOME TO NORMAL. All around us the bare fields stretched seemingly forever. It was fittingly flat outside Normal, which is between Joliet and Peoria. Joliet is where they have a big, bad jail, and Peoria is where this book, for example, won't play. The town of Normal itself is, at first glance, very solid. Main Street has a stationery store, a used furniture store, a new furniture store, a lingerie shop, and several bars. We were directed to a place called the Posh Nosh for lunch. I ordered gumbo. This being the Midwest, gumbo was turkey rice soup with a sliced hot dog in it.

Jeff, a former student of David's who's lived most of his life in Normal, is worried about having it too easy there. "I find it hard to imagine the outside world," he told me. "The Russians won't bomb us, and there is plenty to eat." "That may be so," I said, "but farmers shoot bankers around here, and there are PCBs in the cows." "Well, to me that seems normal," said Jeff. It occurred to me that everything seems normal to those who are raised with it. Nobody's a character to himself, as Ted Berrigan said. It takes an outsider's eye to see the abnormal in the seemingly natural.

David and I went into the new furniture store. "I bought a couch and a chair here two years ago," David said loudly, "and termites came out of them. They've collapsed the whole east wing of my house!" "My God!" screamed the salesman. Two shoppers started edging toward the door. "Only kidding, folks!" said David. They wouldn't listen. The worm of doubt born of fantasy had entered the minds of the shoppers of Normal.

At the lingerie store David asked for musical underwear. "Never heard of it," said the rosy-cheeked salesgirl. Our laughter froze in our throats seconds later when, as we emerged onto

Main Street, we saw two workers in overalls about to jump from the roof of the bank building. "DON'T!" we shouted in unison. The workers didn't move. We looked closer and saw that they were really only super-realistic sculptures, as good as any by New York practitioners of the genre.

They're still laughing at us in Normal.

Palm Beach Dog Bar
and Chafing Dish

"Look at that!" exclaimed Rose. "It's not even good material! And look at the shabby workmanship!" She dismissed with a contemptuous wave of her hand all the extravagantly priced wares of Gucci, Ralph Lauren, Christina, and Vuitton. And as final proof of a world of misplaced values, she showed me a little blue faience shrine filled with water, sticking out into the overdressed street. Above it, in large painted letters, were the words DOG BAR. After, or maybe before, buying their Gucci shoes and Vuitton socks, the oligarchy of Palm Beach, Florida, brings their poodles here, to drink at this DOG BAR.

Rose has real values, and she knows her materials and her workmanship. In the 1930s she worked in New York's garment district. She now lives in a large retirement community in West Palm Beach, a city unto itself really, and leads a campaign to keep the libraries there full of books. The old folks like to read, in spite of, or perhaps because of, the unaffordable world next door. Her community, Century Village, the Sunbelt's largest village of the old (population 20,000), counts among its residents folks who try to make it exclusively on Social Security. "So it's no wonder," says Rose, "that they sometimes slip an apple or a banana into their bags at the store when no one's looking. Hunger is alive and well in Paradise!"

In the midst of Florida's economic boom in the salad days of Reaganism, books are faring even worse than the poor. Austerity budgets are being felt by every public library. I tell Rose that in New Orleans the library's budget is always the first one cut. Branch libraries are all going to close unless something is done fast.

With a passion born way back in the heyday of the Garment Workers' Union, Rose says, "My books are my children!" An immeasurably sweet feeling of civilization exudes from that phrase. We are not just losing books when we lose libraries; we lose all possibility of the continuance of culture.

Keep 'em honest in Shangri-la, Rose!

Prospero-Paranoia

"What do you think about the new prosperity?" Colin Covert asked me in Minneapolis.

"The what?" I said. "I live in Louisiana. We don't have that there."

"Well," Colin explained, "it's everywhere else. You look over your head and see stock speculators high on money gas colliding with one another between brand-new skyscrapers."

I looked up: there they were, their high-tech balloons shiny with bathos.

"In Louisiana," I said, "you can see grown men in slightly worn suits rolling empty oil barrels down the deserted streets with big sticks. Former millionaires are subsistence-fishing off abandoned wharfs, but all they catch are huge chunks of toxic waste they once threw in there."

"The new prosperity is a very skittish thing," said Colin. "Everybody's high here but *nervous*. I call it prospero-paranoia."

Minneapolis is a clean city. There wasn't a single newspaper littering the wide, well-scrubbed, tastefully unpopulated sidewalks. Everyone was either flying overhead or inside the malls, shopping. The latest political scandal in the state had to do with a bribery case in which thirty-five dollars' worth of Twinkies had been distributed to voters by the campaign staff of a candidate for the City Council. For trying to bribe his way into office, the candidate was sentenced to two days in jail. Yes, Twinkies continue to loom large in the nation's psyche.

Here in Louisiana our governor was discovered to have handed suitcases full of cash to guys from Las Vegas in the lobbies of hotels where he was registered under a false name. The citizens were polled for their opinion. "He didn't do anything wrong," they opined, "so long as it was his own money."

Indeed. Where style is concerned, there are Twinkies and there are twinkies. Meanwhile, the nervous prospero-paranoids of Minneapolis avoided mid-air collisions between the ever-growing skyscrapers as the sidewalks got fuller. I couldn't live with the increasing tension. I hopped a plane home. Broke out my fishing rod. Started typing this.

Citizen of the Hyatt

I spent three days in the Hyatt House in Indianapolis recently, and I have come back to report that it can support human life indefinitely. Its climate very much resembles that of earth. There are green plants hanging from protruding formations, and once I stumbled into a circle of extremely real-looking potted shrubs around a black piano. Seated there was somebody who mightily resembled a pianist making something that sounded like music. Strewn about in formations of two and three, realistic couples sipped liquid from tall glasses and nodded plesantly at each other.

The air is neither too thin nor too thick and is slightly scented by the thousands of bodies scrubbed with hotel soap that stumble out of its showers every morning. I had a good look at the city of Indianapolis out the window of my room, and the air outside appeared to my naked eye to be cold, crisp, and turbulent. I experienced none of those conditions behind the plate-glass window that separated me from the city. I would have liked to go out there to walk around but I immediately suppressed that nostalgic impulse by reminding myself that thanks to modern art, which isolates the eyes from all the other senses, I could now safely view the world without actually mucking about in it.

The most remarkable aspect of the Hyatt is the supportive nutritive system. On several floors discreet little feeding stations functioned smoothly. All of them produced several varieties of nachos, Bloody Marys, and fried zucchini. The ones on the lower floors also stacked large slabs of recently killed meat, so that I became convinced that an advanced system of communication existed between the Hyatt and the outside world.

As I rose silently in the glass bubbles of the elevators, I

surveyed the seemingly endless tiers of this immaculately ordered world. In one large room, businessmen stood before gadgets with drinks in their hands. In another large room, writers read poems to appreciative audiences with pockets bulging with their own poems. This was the room where I too was expected. I pulled the paper from my pocket. At the top it said, "Hyatt, the Perfect World." I began to read.

Amsterdam

I was perched atop a stool in the loft of a pirate radio station in Amsterdam talking with Bill Levy about Ollie North and other pressing matters. "Occasionally the police raid us," Bill said casually. They didn't raid us then, nor were they around when we met up with Stefan, an East German who publishes books in Holland, at one of the city's many tea shops sporting a marijuana leaf on their signs. Stefan deliberated in front of the menu: "Colombian? Nigerian? Sensa?" The different grades were different prices, too. Grass wasn't my cup of tea, so after Stefan made his purchase I got some herring with a slice of raw onion on a bun from a street vendor.

Like the herring, everything about Amsterdam is sea-salty and bracing. At the corner of Bill's house on one of the smaller canals we discoursed with the salty Ten-Finger Eddy, the King of the Red Light District. Ten-Finger Eddy had just buried his dog Shnoofy in Amsterdam's pet cemetery in five lots topped with a specially built marble monument. He'd had a New Orleans jazz band see Shnoofy off, and there were posters all over the city: SHNOOFY'S STILL WATCHING! Later we went to the Aorta, a skinhead club filled with perfect punks, including a guy dressed in spikes and leather on one side of his person, lace and makeup on the other. Next morning, I watched the good burghers of Amsterdam go to their bountiful markets, where the sensible prices are marked clearly (taxes included), and felt the pleasure that Vermeer and Brueghel felt in the steady commonness of their fellows. While every other painter in Europe was painting princes and court scenes, the Dutch were depicting the common folk and the lovely things they ate.

Since everyone in Amsterdam speaks English, there was little incentive for me to penetrate the strangeness of the Dutch language, which stared at me from billboards with the thousand eyes of its double o's. Bill has been living in Holland for fifteen years, Stefan for almost as long. It's easy to see why.

Paris, France

A guy burst into the métro car and proceeded to bang on his guitar. "OK, all right!" he said in English, "I wrote this song this morning!" And he let out an indescribable chant in French. Most riders smiled even as they covered their ears. At the end of his gruesome ballad, which had to do, as far as I was able to make it out, with getting up that very morning and dreaming about being in the métro, everybody handed him a franc. Instead of calling the police or roughing him up, that is. Outside the métro was an impersonator doing what I thought was Richard Nixon. Impersonators are odd beings. I can't stand them ever since one walked behind me for a full minute and everybody laughed at me.

Paris makes you think of impersonators and ventriloquists. Maybe it's Picasso's harlequins, or the circus paintings of the Impressionists, but they are everywhere. In fact, most of the boulevard fauna in the City of Light was being something other than what it was, which was elegant French people out for a walk. Young folks on the Boulevard Saint Germain were impersonating Americans of the same age. They wore T-shirts with English words on them, only the words didn't exactly jibe: "Snake Valley Universal Games," "Virginia University Team Football," "K of E Alright," and this, whatever *it* means: "Hippies Keep Off of SNOBBISH and Hysterics Et Vous." You figure it.

Sitting at the Deux Magots with a fifty-dollar peewee cup of coffee, I kept wishing for the dollar seventy-five BBQ sandwich and clam chowder *plus* coffee at Tammy's Café back home, and thinking about what a plain hick I'd become in the few years that I'd been making America my home. I didn't even care for all the splendid fashions and intrigue of the perfumed evening, or for the buildings that had so finely frozen centuries of ideas in their well-turned bodies. Nor did I much care for the intense social interaction that had everybody checking out everybody else, causing them to shake like wet dogs with all the excitement they'd picked up staring too long at each others' seams and outlines. The café was like a pooch convention on a rug filled with static. I felt like standing instead on a ball field among children dressed in identical baseball uniforms sponsored by the hardware store and Tammy's Café, having a Pepsi.

Topless beauties were bathing on both shores of the Seine amid the elegant shadows of kings' statues, and I was dreaming of skinny- dipping in the Mississippi. A suicidal thought, especially in New Orleans. True, there were a lot of people with books in the little parks of Paris where the birds are not afraid, and for a moment all the doomed beauty of Europe flooded me with a different set of clichés. But that Europe was, alas, on the wane. There were lines around the block at McDonald's, and the burgers cost a fortune.

The French philosopher E. M. Cioran told me in a voice weary with the wisdom of centuries of European history: "If the Americans pull back, Europe is finished. The Russians are only a few hundred kilometers from Paris." Having lived through two world wars and then some, Cioran's weariness was hardly ideological. He was stating what looked to him obvious. Pointing to the spires of Notre Dame in the sunset he said, "In the year 2000, Notre Dame will be a mosque." I laughed, but he didn't.

Living in America has almost cured me of my intrinsic cynicism which, for a European from a small nation, is a birthright. This cynicism is a defense against a history too often cruel, and a foil for those who would use utopia to promise things that never materialize. In shedding it, I have become younger. American faith in the future is contagious. It makes one instantly young. But the young, as everyone knows, can be foolish as well as dangerous.

I asked Cioran if he had ever been to America. "Oh, no," he replied, "I am a provincial of the Quarter" (the Latin Quarter of

Paris). Some other provincials of this place had been Voltaire, Sartre, and Trotsky. As I watched the life swirling about me, I tried to feel the lingering power of this cultural vortex. It was there even as the surface was made of signs from elsewhere. The young people in their touching American clothes did not perhaps want to be Americans. What they wanted was some of America's young energy, its optimism. Weary like Cioran of the bitter lessons of Europe, they merely wanted to be young.

The Tourist

S uddenly the tourist is the central figure of our time. Attacked by terrorists, defended by the U.S. Sixth Fleet, the tourist emerges from his baffled Bermuda shorts into the limelight of world politics.

But the tourist has always been there. The Japanese may have perfected the current version of him, but he goes back much further and is synonymous with British colonialism. First came the conquering armies, then the little people with the sketchbooks and the cameras. Natives have always hated tourists, and tourists have always done their best to understand nothing about the natives. But hatred begins at home: tourists are barely tolerated even when touring their own countries. Just think of your own resentful bemusement at the sight of busloads of strange Americans in your favorite hangout in your hometown. Unchecked, the tourist will climb over the fence and come right into your house to take pictures of you in your habitat. Cities mindful of tourists have built elaborate "tourist traps" which, luckily, work. Tourists are kept confined to these, and few escape. There is, of course, the type known as the "intrepid tourist." This one has to be watched carefully or he can become most annoying. Little wonder these are so often the target of terrorists.

If there is an aspect of benign terror about the tourist, there is also a great deal of tourist in the terrorist. Terrorists travel with only one thing in mind, just like the tourist, and the specifics of places escape them both. Terrorists travel for the purpose of shooting unsuspecting foreigners, just as tourists travel for the purpose of shooting them with a camera. You could say that a terrorist is a tourist with a gun and a tourist is a terrorist with a camera.

Clearly, there is a fundamental difference. Guns kill people, while cameras merely steal their souls. But in a war of symbols, things do tend to change places.

Time on the Cuff

T here was this guy in the Newark airport wearing three watches on each of his arms. I asked him what time it was. "That depends," he said. "In London it's four o'clock. In Beijing it's eleven." "In New York?" I said. "I wouldn't know," he said, disgusted.

I could see his point. The man was a dreamer. Anyone can find out what time it is where he lives, but what's the point? It's only useful if you want to go to work or watch TV. On the other hand, time is interesting in places where one isn't: they might be making love or sleeping in Beijing while in London they might be rioting. Everything happens where one isn't, and in a certain time that isn't now.

I've always been intrigued by those airport clocks and weather maps that display the numbers of elsewhere. They are a guarantee of difference while being, at the same time, a reiteration of the fact that the world is round. It's nice to live in a world that's all one but at the same time all different. What more could one want in terms of community? Well, a little slack, for one thing. I wouldn't mind time if I didn't have to consult a clock so often.

When I was thirteen my big birthday present was a watch. Every five years since, my parents have given me a new one. They've gotten increasingly sophisticated, these timepieces, in addition to coming in ever more attractive shapes with nicer wristbands. Yet I've never changed how I feel about them: I've never worn them, and I'm not wearing one now. Most people, I know, don't even need the fancy watches they sport: time is in their blood, beating. It's their pulse. It's what speeds up when they're called up for duty, which is more and more often. It's the new factory whistle and it lives in us.

But then, even as the world we know becomes the body of a huge clock surrounded by a fancy cover, there are dreamers like the guy in Newark and refuseniks, like me, who'd rather ask time from a guy keeping track of London and Beijing.

It took you about two minutes to read this.

Alligators

T here is a drainage ditch behind the inexpensive student housing in back of LSU. It's filled with beer cans. I was watching it in the mid-morning heat in something like the way a visitor to a museum watches a big trash sculpture, when the whole mess moved and the green-gray back of a large alligator slowly slid into view. Slowly, it then slid back out of it. Later I was told that the students know him well. They threaten to throw themselves to him if they don't make their exams.

On one side of the canal is a nursery school, closed down now for the summer. On the other, a dog lay prostrated on his back, his tongue hanging way out of his mouth. Alligators are somehow indispensable to this tropical lassitude. They go with the bananas and the figs in my backyard. They like to imitate logs and move as little as possible. There is probably one treading water in the sewer back of the house as I lie here in my hammock with my mouth open, waiting for a ripe fig to fall off the tree into it.

Living with large reptiles is an acquired taste, I'm sure, but I'm acquiring it in a hurry. Had alligator several times now. Yep, it *does* taste like chicken. How did you know? Actually it tastes like frog-fish. Had shark too, and other barely mentionables. I'll have 'em again too, if I ever get out of this hammock.

When you sway in a hammock in August in Louisiana, you can see the concentric waves of heat shimmering and throwing back colors. If you hear music it's because it drifts in on the heat from radios in other hammocks under other banana and fig trees. Of course nobody works. The alligator is the model for both behavior and fashion. Move as little as possible and stay green and deep down. If you have to get up, invent a reason why you can't. If you're hungry, open your mouth and wait for food to fall into it. If you drink, drink gin and tonic or mint julep. Keep your eyes half lidded and let the flowers perfume your somnolence. The world is a dream and you're a half-sleeping alligator, stupidly treading water down in it.

Vacation Angst

T wo elderly tourists stood in front of the Storyville jazz club in New Orleans shuffling slightly. It was an extraordinary shuffle because they both put as much gusto into it as their acute sense of social embarrassment would allow—and they were only shuffling *slightly*. I mean, if you hadn't been watching as closely as I was, from the window of the sweltering café across the street, you might have mistaken the shuffle for a walking peculiarity. They were both holding the ubiquitous New Orleans "go cups" in their hands, so you knew they'd already had a few and had shed quite a few inhibitions to get that wild. Written in that shuffle was the tragic double-story of vacation and retirement. Here they were, both retired and on vacation, letting loose, but it was clear that they just couldn't remember how. The shuffle itself was like a painful memory from college days fifty years before. The steps were hesitant and ancient.

"Thank God," said my friend, "that life is my only job. There is no retirement from *that*!"

My friend takes her job seriously; she would never retire her shuffle to mince steps for an employer. Most people, however, put their dancing shoes on ice when they start punching the clock. Fifty years later here they are, shuffling slightly in memory of their youth. I could feel their *angst* blowing in the open window of the café like a breeze of workaday sorrow. It was a cool evening in the "city that care forgot," but cares blew about anyway like old newspapers.

Vacations are desperate things even if you are not old and retired. I have always felt keenly the unbearable pathos of tourism, the lonely masses of the twentieth century shuffling through each others' cities in small, insulated units looking for innocence. It's there somewhere, riddled with the holes the clock punched in it.

When the couple shuffled off into the night, the café owner closed the windows and turned on the air conditioner.

The Whites of Their Eyes

T he nights are getting so crisp you can hear the banana leaves moan on their stalks. There is a dense gold in the light as it falls on the wrought iron fences in the French Quarter. Huddled in the chill coming off the lake, duck hunters stand behind their blinds watching the sky darken. Some of them have gotten their shotguns free from the local Ford dealer who'd been giving one away with every pickup. Yep, you buy a pickup, you get a shotgun.

A little to the south of us, in Florida, where the nights are shorter but the air conditioners still hum, they've passed a new gun law that practically makes it incumbent upon every citizen to wear a pistol. As if every citizen didn't already have a pistol. Or two, or eight. Every time somebody's car gets broken into, the thief takes a pistol out of the glove compartment. Every time a woman looks through her purse, she first has to get around the gun in there to find whatever she's looking for. Now and again a child gets blasted by the loaded revolver under his mattress. Not *every* pistol goes off. But every mattress hides one.

A European friend of mine came to visit a while ago. All he wanted to do was buy a gun because he couldn't believe you could just walk into a store and buy one. He bought a gun. It made his day. I took him to a sporting goods store here that makes the arsenals of most small countries look pitiful. The ceiling of this place is festooned with antique Colts and Remingtons. Every inch of wall is covered with rifles, shotguns, and carbines. A huge stuffed bear with two holes in his head stands by the door. Until a few years ago they had a sign under one of the guns here that said THE RIFLE THAT KILLED KENNEDY.

The right to bear arms is no misnomer: we bear them and bear them. It's our cross. You can hear the *poppop* of duck hunters where I type. And the *whoosh* of tires as new pickups grip the road. And the locks that lock when someone comes in or goes out. And the longer night following the shorter day, the armed night following the armored day.

About the Author

Andrei Codrescu is a poet, translator, and editor. He teaches English at Louisiana State University in Baton Rouge, and edits *Exquisite Corpse*, a monthly review of books and ideas. His commentaries on books and culture can be heard on National Public Radio.